MW01206303

Squirrels

Squirrels

GEORGE LAYCOCK

FOUR WINDS PRESS   NEW YORK

LIBRARY OF CONGRESS CATALOGING IN PUBLICATION DATA

Laycock, George.
  Squirrels.

  SUMMARY: Discusses the characteristics and behavior of and
many little-known facts about squirrels and such cousins of theirs
as the chipmunk, woodchuck, sik-sik, and prairie dog.
  1. Squirrels—Juvenile literature. [1. Squirrels]
I. Title.
QL737.R68L39   599'.3232   74–28478
ISBN 0–590–07376–1

PUBLISHED BY FOUR WINDS PRESS
A DIVISION OF SCHOLASTIC MAGAZINES, INC., NEW YORK, N.Y.
COPYRIGHT © 1975 BY GEORGE LAYCOCK

LIBRARY OF CONGRESS CATALOG CARD NUMBER: 74–28478

1 2 3 4 5   79 78 77 76 75

PHOTO CREDITS

Luther C. Goldman, Bureau of Sport Fisheries and Wildlife, p. 87
Karl H. Maslowski, pp. 42, 46, 49, 51, 53, 57, 59, 71, 75, 78, 86
Peter and Stephen Maslowski, p. 69
National Park Service, p. 39
All other photographs are by the author.

ACKNOWLEDGMENTS

The author wishes to express his thanks to all who helped during the preparation of this book. For help in supplying illustrations, photographer Karl H. Maslowski and the U.S. Fish and Wildlife Service deserve special mention. Mr. and Mrs. James J. Dallis, who shared their home with Frisky and Whiskers, were especially helpful.

CONTENTS

The old mother squirrel at the entrance to her home in the cherry tree.

Chapter one

~~~~~~~~~~~~~~~~~~~~~~~~~~~~~~~~~~

SQUIRREL WATCHING

In the early morning sun the old mother squirrel sits peacefully above the entrance to her home in the hollow wild cherry tree. I wonder what she is doing. The answer is that she is just sitting, as we've seen her do many times in the years she has lived in the cherry tree. Nobody can blame a squirrel for this, especially an old squirrel that has run hard through the treetops for many years.

For several minutes she stays there as if she is still sleepy. Her long bushy tail, as wide as her body, curves up over her back like a narrow blanket for her to hide beneath. Her eyes are half closed. Nothing seems to worry her this morning. No dog runs through her woods. No red-tailed hawk cruises overhead. No man is out yet. This old mother squirrel seems to be the most contented gray squirrel in the world.

After a while she moves. One hind foot comes up and she scratches beneath her neck. Her foot moves so fast it becomes a blur of fur and claws. She turns her head and carefully licks the hair on her shoulder. Then she stretches and steps off the limb where she rested. She begins running head first down the rough black side of the big cherry tree.

Halfway to the ground she stops and looks around. Every tree

1

and living creature in her woods is known to her. She has lived here long enough to know what is dangerous to her.

Two bluejays fly into the woods and perch in the top of a big oak tree above her. She glances up at them. Their noisy calls sometimes are a warning of danger. But the squirrel sees no danger and she is soon running down the tree again.

She gains speed, running flat against the bark, head first. Her sharp claws dig into the bark like hooks, and at every step they keep her hanging safely on the tree far above the earth.

Then, near the ground, she leaps as easily as a young squirrel out onto the forest floor. The brown, dead leaves crackle under her feet. She walks a few feet. Her pointed nose is close to the ground and she sniffs among the leaves, exploring the hillside. She makes a few long graceful hops and stops each time to sniff the leaves again. But she does not find what she is searching for. She does not stop to dig, but only sniffs. She finds no treasures buried beneath the leaves this morning.

Her search brings her to the base of a tall oak tree. With a springing leap she clamps her feet to the side of the tree and begins climbing toward the clouds. Each step is a little jump straight up along the tree trunk, and whenever her long toes touch the shaggy bark her sharp claws dig in and hold her there. Quickly her strong hind legs push her far up into the treetop.

The treetop is a special world. The squirrel looks down and sees us walking in the woods far below. Sure-footed and nimble, it scampers along the limbs, then leaps out of one tree and into the next. It can travel through the forest without coming to the ground. And when it stops to look around, what a view it has! It can see over the tops of the trees, beyond the roof of our house, and across the whole neighborhood.

Up there against the sky the squirrels play together. Like acrobats playing tag on a tightwire, they run as fast as they can along

SQUIRRELS

slender limbs. Or they scamper up and down the tree trunk, chasing each other around and around the tree on their way down to the ground, then back up to their leafy platform in the treetops.

Finally, the old squirrel runs nimbly out on the big crooked limb which she follows every morning when she is coming to have breakfast with us. She rushes to the very edge of the limb. The twigs bend beneath her weight. Then she leaps across open space. If she missed, she would fall fifty feet straight down to the ground. But she does not miss. Instead she lands on the tips of the branches of a shagbark hickory tree.

Through this tree she travels as fast as her legs will carry her, and then leaps again. This time her jump carries her into the top of a young maple tree that grows right behind the house. Its limbs stretch toward the railing of the deck at the back of the house. This deck is where the old squirrel is always headed at breakfast time.

Once more she leaps through the air and this time she lands on the narrow flat railing of the deck outside our window. Here she is fifteen feet above the ground, where a bird feeder is nailed to the railing. The feeder is covered with cardinals, goldfinches, chickadees, and titmice having their breakfast. But the birds have seen the old squirrel coming through the maple tree, and now, as her feet touch down on the railing, there is a flurry of feathers as all the birds fly into the nearby trees. They sit there watching the squirrel as she feasts on sunflower seeds. She has chased them off and there is nothing they can do about this.

The old mother squirrel is only one of many squirrels in the woods behind the house. All of them come through the trees to the bird feeder sometime during the winter day. But no other squirrel comes while the old one sits there among the seeds. If they try it, she rushes at them angrily and chases them off to wait until she has eaten as much as she wants.

These three squirrels come regularly to our winter bird feeding station.

For two years after the bird feeder was placed there, the squirrels could not figure out how they could get to its wealth of good things. They would sit on the branches of the maple tree and study the feeder hungrily. But the tree was still too small and the distance from the longest limbs to the feeder too great to risk. I think it was the old mother squirrel who first solved the problem.

She came to the young maple tree one afternoon as I watched. There she tilted and balanced high above the ground like a trapeze artist. Her feet moved about in a little dance step as she shifted her weight. Her broad tail helped keep her balanced while her head moved back and forth as she tried to make up her mind whether to leap or not.

From this location she watched the cardinals as they came to eat. She saw the little chickadees with their black caps and the titmice with their sharp, gray crests. But the limb swayed so much beneath her that she could not jump.

That night, she lay curled snug and warm inside her den in the old cherry tree. Outside, a cold west wind whispered through the naked trees while a soft snow sifted into the dark forest. But in the morning she was out of her tree house early while I was still in bed.

The first gray light of dawn was turning the forest trees into dark shadows against the new snow as she ran quickly down from her cherry tree. I have watched her do it many times since. She leaped from its trunk and sniffed at the brown, snow-crusted leaves on the wooded hillside, until she came to the edge of the woods. She lifted her head and her beady eyes searched carefully for the dogs that sometimes come to the woods. If she is in her tree when the dogs arrive, she scolds them and twitches her long tail angrily as if daring them to come up the tree and get her. But on the ground she becomes uneasy. She keeps a constant watch and at the first sign of danger dashes for the nearest tree and safety.

But no dog was around, or any owl or hawk or human being, and she felt safe. She ran in long graceful leaps across the yard to the front of the house. There she scurried up an ash tree and ran out on a limb until the roof of the house was only a few feet beneath her.

I awakened when I heard the gentle thump and then the racing feet on the roof, crossing the top of the house.

The old squirrel came to the back of the house. She leaned out from the edge of the roof. The ground was far below. But between her and the ground was the bird feeder nailed to the railing on the deck. She edged out for a good look at the sunflower seeds. Then she was hanging by her hind feet and in this way she moved down over the edge of the roof so she could touch the downspout.

This spout reached straight down the side of the house, and paint on it made the surface rough enough for her to grip with her feet. She climbed skillfully down the pipe until, with a little plop, she landed on the deck railing. Then she had only to walk along the railing to the bird feeder.

I came to the back window just in time to see her scare all the birds from the sunflower seeds. She sat upright in the middle of the feeder looking at me. We were only a few feet from each other, but she did not leave. For the old squirrel this was a feast, and she was dipping her mouth into the seeds and eating as fast as she could. She held her paws up beside her mouth as she ate. Empty hulls of sunflower seeds fell steadily from both sides of her mouth.

Now that the old mother squirrel knew the route, she came often. She usually joined us at breakfast or lunch. While we ate on one side of the window, she ate happily on the other.

In addition, her young squirrels soon learned to follow her. Often three or four squirrels were having breakfast around the bird feeder at the same time. The old mother would take her place in the feeder. The others would settle for the "table scraps" kicked to

6

the floor of the deck by her fast-moving feet.

At first the squirrels at the feeder departed by the same route they followed to get there—up the downspout, then across the roof to the front yard. They would then have to run back around the house to the back yard. For several years the young maple tree grew steadily, and the old mother squirrel was the first to use this new route through its branches to the feeder.

Usually the squirrels did not worry about us as long as we stayed inside the house. But the instant the sliding door opened, all squirrels would scamper from the deck in a panic and take off directly toward the ground.

This time, I took one step onto the deck and the old squirrel's head jerked up. Her long tail twitched and she chattered at me angrily. She turned and faced the woods and gathered all four feet like springs beneath her furry body. She had her eyes fixed on a little maple limb no thicker than a pencil.

Never before had we seen any squirrel attempt to leap directly into the maple tree behind the house. But suddenly the old mother squirrel launched herself into the crisp winter air, in a magnificent broad jump. All four feet were spread wide and her long tail flowed out behind her. It was the performance of a wild champion. She leaped across five feet of space far above the ground, and hit the little limb right on target.

She swung beneath the limb, clinging with all four feet. The limb bent deeply toward the earth, then lifted again. She was still angry with me. She climbed into the tree and sat there, chattering and scolding me, her tail twitching and her long, orange-colored front teeth showing.

When her circus act began, I thought she might plunge to earth. Although gray squirrels almost never fall out of trees, it can happen. One day I watched two squirrels scampering through the trees as fast as they could race. Their courting game took them twisting and turning onto new limbs, spiraling up and around tree trunks, then speeding along toward the end of a long branch on a giant oak tree.

The squirrel in front hesitated, and the other squirrel bumped into it. They both slipped and all eight feet were grabbing for limbs they could not hold, and both squirrels were plunging out of the treetop.

Their fall began sixty feet above the forest floor. Many animals falling such a distance would hit the earth with a sickening thud and die there. The falling squirrels were stretching and reaching wildly for every branch as they sped past. Then, halfway down, one of them caught a branch and quickly twisted and grasped it with all four feet, upside down until he could crawl to safety.

Its companion, however, was not so fortunate. All four feet were spread wide and its long tail fanned out straight behind it as it plummeted toward the earth. It struck the leaf-covered ground, rolled over, bounced, and landed on its feet again. It shook its head once and rushed at top speed to the trunk of the tree. A minute later both squirrels were back where their fall had interrupted them, unhurt and chasing each other wildly through the treetops again.

A friend of mine put up a bird feeder on a metal pipe set in the ground. It was five feet above the ground. Surely it would be out of reach of the squirrels. But squirrels soon began climbing straight up the pipe and over the bottom of the feeder to get inside.

One day the squirrels had a big surprise. The first squirrel of the morning made a running start across the yard toward the bird feeder and hit the pole about a foot above ground. It started to climb, but instead of going up, the squirrel came back down. It bounced against the ground and promptly tried again. Each time the results were the same. There was nothing it could do—the

Hanging upside down by its hind feet, this squirrel takes sunflower seeds from the bird feeder.

pipe had been greased with Vaseline. The hungry squirrel had to go to the woods and search for buried acorns.

The next winter, as the old mother squirrel and her family came and went easily from the trees to the bird feeder, I waited for the first ice storm. By now the maple limbs had grown bigger and stronger and all the squirrels in the woods had learned to leap skillfully from the tree and land neatly right beside the feeder on the railing of the deck. None of them any longer had to run around the house and across the roof.

The ice storm came in the middle of a December night. In the early morning the radio warned that people going to work should drive with extreme caution. School buses did not run because schools were closed. On such a morning, perhaps the old mother squirrel would stay in her cherry tree. Squirrels often stay in their nests during winter storms.

In an ice storm the whole woods turns to a million icicles. Cold rains falling against the trees build up layers of glistening ice. Every limb becomes brittle. The ice blankets all surfaces of the deck, especially the railing. Only one thing could possibly happen if the old mother squirrel should land on that railing when it was covered with ice. It would be a hard lesson for her, and we worried about her having a crash landing.

At breakfast I turned every few minutes to look into the icy woods. Then I saw her stick her little gray head from the hole in the tree and sniff the cold air. She eased out onto the tree and was soon running along the limbs easily.

She followed her usual highway through the trees toward the house. She eased out onto the ice-covered maple limb and paused there, moving her head back and forth as if studying the situation. Surely this experienced old squirrel would not be fool enough to risk such a leap and end up sliding all around the deck.

But she did. In an instant she was airborne. Then all four feet hit the ice with a tinkling musical sound. I did not believe what I

A gray squirrel and his supply of pignut
hickories on a log in the autumn woods.

saw. She didn't slide or tumble head over furry tail. Instead she
came to a sudden halt at the end of her jump as if all four feet
were nailed to the railing. She turned to the fresh supply of sunflower seeds as if there was nothing to make this morning any
different from all the others. And there she sat, staring through the
glass at me with her big dark eyes, as she hungrily stuffed sunflower seeds into her mouth.

One late autumn day we had a special treat for the old squirrel.
We had been to visit friends in the country and when we returned
I had a sweater pocketful of big, solid hickory nuts.

Our hickory trees had not grown many nuts, and those that did
appear were taken by the squirrels while the nuts were still soft
and green. It had been a long time since the squirrels had tasted a
hickory nut such as those I carried home.

On Thanksgiving morning I remembered my old sweater. The

hickory nuts were still in the pocket. I placed one of the big hickory nuts beside the bird feeder. The first squirrel down that morning was the old mother squirrel from the cherry tree. As usual she went straight to work on the sunflower seeds. Her pointed face dipped down into the pile of gray and white seeds, then jerked back up. There she sat on her haunches, holding the seeds in her mouth with the sides of her paws.

Then her round dark eyes spied the strange hickory nut. The sunflower seeds could wait. She moved toward the hickory nut, sniffing all the way. She picked the big nut up in her jaws. Then she dug into a corner of the bird feeder and placed the hickory nut in the pile of seeds. Using her front paws she pulled some seeds over it. She patted them down a couple of times until her new treasure was completely buried out of sight beneath the sunflower seeds.

She seemed to forget the nut and began eating sunflower seeds again. After a few minutes, her breakfast finished, she leaped into the maple tree and began running along the limbs toward her cherry tree. But about halfway home she stopped. She turned and looked back at the house and the bird feeder as if she had forgotten something.

Then she rushed back down through the trees and made her usual beautiful leap to the deck railing. Did she want more sunflower seeds? Not this time. She went sniffing to the corner where the hickory nut was hidden. Quickly she dug it out. She was on her way again, carrying in her mouth as fine a hickory nut as she had ever seen.

Halfway home she stopped for lunch. Sitting on a limb, her tail curled up over her back, she began cutting into the nut. The old mother from the cherry tree had a special Thanksgiving treat that morning. Later I put out the other hickory nuts and all the squirrels helped finish them.

Chapter two

GRAY SQUIRRELS

There are several hundred kinds of squirrels around the world. They live wild on every continent except Australia. Within the squirrel family there are tree squirrels, ground squirrels, and flying squirrels.

The most widely known of the American tree squirrels is the gray squirrel. In the eastern United States the gray squirrel belongs to the hardwood forests. The western gray squirrel lives in the oaks and pines in western parts of Washington, Oregon, and California.

Gray squirrels really belong in the deep forests. Before settlers came to the eastern shores of North America, tall trees crowded together everywhere, keeping the earth in dark, cool shadows. This wilderness stretched on and on, a home for bears, deer, elk, wolves, cougars, and wild turkeys. And the green leaves shook beneath the scurrying feet of millions of squirrels.

People saw their tails twitching in the treetops everywhere. Some called the gray squirrel "silvertail." Others knew them as bannertails or shadetails. The Chippewa Indians called this squirrel "ah-ji-duh-mo," which meant "tail in the air."

The gray squirrels were so numerous that soon they became the enemies of the settlers. Let a man clear a field and grow a crop,

An adult gray squirrel running along a log.

and squirrels would come swarming from the forest to eat his grain. In Pennsylvania, in 1749, a bounty was paid on squirrels. Each squirrel was worth a three pence reward when brought in dead. Ohio citizens paid part of their taxes in dead squirrels. This, however, was not enough to stop the squirrels.

Meanwhile the woodcutters were busy chopping the trees down. There were now open fields where the forests had been, and some wild animals had lost their homes. Because the trees were disappearing so were wild turkeys, bears, and deer. And by the time of the Civil War there were not nearly so many gray squirrels as there once had been. But the forests were still being cut and burned, and the ground was left smoking and bare where the trees had stood.

By 1900 some people were worried about the eastern gray squirrels. They thought that these sleek little animals of the tree-tops might become extinct. But gradually the forests began to come back, and so did the squirrels.

A gray squirrel is about eighteen inches long. Take away his fine long tail, however, and he is only ten inches long. The adult weighs about one pound.

The gray squirrel's sleek, smooth coat often has some brown mixed in with the gray. The brown shows especially on the squirrel's head and sides. Underneath, the squirrel is white. The tail is dark gray with a wide band of white around its edge. The squirrel molts two times each year, once in the spring and once in fall. The old hair falls out a little at a time and in its place new hair grows. By early winter the squirrel wears a fine new fur coat to lock in its body heat through the cold months. It keeps its coat in condition by licking itself or by taking a dust bath. All members of the family look so much alike that there is no way to tell males from females or young from old by the color of their coats.

How does the squirrel climb so well? The secret is in the design of its feet. It has long slender toes, four on each front foot, and five on the rear, and each toe has a curved nail with a sharp point. Its toes are tree hooks, and when the squirrel sets one of its feet against the bark, those sharp curved claws dig in and hold fast.

Gray squirrels have excellent vision. The eyes, framed in a ring of white fur, are placed so the squirrel can see behind itself without turning its head. It can also see over the top of its head and scan the skies, where a red-tailed hawk may cruise. Or it can see the ground beneath its tree. There is very little going on around it that it cannot see.

A squirrel pausing to wash its face.

Sometimes gray squirrels in the treetops can be heard talking among themselves in soft, chuckling calls. But when they become angry or alarmed, they raise their voices and the scolding of the squirrels rings through the forest. This call is a sharp note and they repeat it rapidly as if barking at the intruders. Or they may start with a loud note and let the sound die away until it is gradually lost in the whispering green leaves.

It is thought that squirrels can hear well. They hear each other call and chatter and bark. And even when mother squirrels are on the ground or in the nest tree, they hear their babies call in their high-pitched, squeaky voices.

In addition, squirrels have teeth that are excellent for chewing through the hard shells of hickory nuts or cutting twigs to build their nests. The long, curved front teeth are called "incisors," and the squirrel has two pairs of them in the front of its mouth. The dark orange outer part, the enamel, is hard, while the inner side of the teeth is softer. This softer, inner part wears away first and leaves a razor-sharp edge of enamel that can carve nut shells or cut deeply into the fingers of anyone who picks up a squirrel. Unlike the teeth of people, a squirrel's teeth continue to grow throughout its life and the squirrel must keep them worn off or they would become so long the squirrel could no longer eat.

That long and beautiful tail is more than decoration to a squirrel. When the squirrel leaps, its tail becomes a rudder to help guide it. If it should fall, the tail spreads out and acts almost like a parachute. When it rains, the tail is curled out and over the back like an umbrella. It is also a sun shade beneath which the squirrel sometimes rests. In the nest it curls around the squirrel and becomes a blanket. If the squirrel goes swimming, its tail stretches out behind it on the water and helps it stay afloat. Besides, squirrels send messages by twitching their tails. They flick them up and down to signal danger to each other when there are enemies nearby.

Another way they have of protecting themselves is to stay very still. Often a squirrel will stop suddenly on the side of a tree, hanging on right where it stopped. No part of the animal seems to move. Only if you are very close will you see its sides moving gently as it breathes. It may stay there "frozen" to the tree for several minutes. An animal is much easier to see when it is moving, and if there is a cat or person in the woods, the frightened squirrel may not move until the danger is past. When it sees an enemy the squirrel may inch around to the far side of its tree and hide there out of sight.

The gray squirrel's sense of smell is excellent. Its nose helps it find buried winter food. By sniffing around the forest floor it knows where to dig because it can smell a buried nut. It digs the nut up and sniffs it some more. It can even tell in this way whether the nut is a good one or the shell is empty, all without cutting it open. This saves the hungry squirrel much time and work and shortens the time it must spend on the ground. This can save its life, for the gray squirrel is safest in the trees. On the ground there are more animals that can catch it; foxes, cats, and dogs roam there. Besides, the squirrel cannot see-as far when on the ground as it can from up in the trees. This is why it is important for the squirrel to find its buried food quickly and then hurry back to the safety of the trees.

Gray squirrels do not live on nuts alone. They relish the seeds of maple trees and eat fruits like mulberry and wild cherry. In spring the squirrels feast on the young buds of maple, elm, and oak trees. During the summer squirrels may eat insects. Or they may rob the nest of a robin or wood thrush for a meal of eggs. They may also like corn growing in the farmers' fields. They are fond of mushrooms—in California the western gray squirrels feed heavily on mushrooms and other fungi.

Early one spring I noticed that one young maple tree on the edge of the woods behind the house had several cuts in its bark. Sugar water flowed down the tree trunk from these cuts. The sap that rose to bring new life to the buds at the tips of its branches was escaping because the tree was scarred with dozens of tooth marks. The whole side of the tree that was in the sunlight was moist with the flowing sap. Our squirrels had tapped the maple tree. They came back to it often to climb slowly along the trunk and lap the sweet sugar water from the side of the tree.

18

A squirrel burying nuts in the woods in autumn.

As fall comes, the eastern squirrel's interest turns to hickory nuts, walnuts, beechnuts, acorns and Osage orange. They eat and grow fat. In a good year there are many nuts and acorns left and the squirrel hurries around burying surplus food. This work goes rapidly through the long soft days of autumn. Each nut is buried about an inch deep and earth is pulled over it. A squirrel does not have a favorite place to bury nuts. Instead it buries them near where it finds them, usually one in each hole it digs.

The squirrel soon forgets where it buried the nut, perhaps because it buries so many of them. When the nut gathering is good, a squirrel may hide forty or more beneath the leaves and soil in an hour. Meanwhile other squirrels are also busy burying nuts. The forest floor hides hundreds of them.

Some of these will become winter food for the squirrels. Insects may destroy others. But some will go undiscovered through the winter and germinate and grow, becoming tall trees in the forest some day. Gray squirrels today may live in trees their ancestors planted a hundred years ago.

The gray squirrel stays close to home if it can find enough to eat there. Usually it will not travel more than a quarter of a mile from its nest. Biologists have caught some gray squirrels, put ear tags on them, and moved them as far as three miles, to see what they might do. The tagged squirrels began moving through the treetops, and within a few days they were back in their own trees.

But a squirrel needs about two pounds of food a week. If it cannot find nuts, fruit, or other foods it may move away. Young squirrels that leave the nests in summer sometimes have to move to new homes where the woods are less crowded with squirrels. Old squirrels are believed to drive them away. The young squirrels may travel several miles through the forest until they find a place where there is food to eat and room to live.

When there are many squirrels and not much food, the squirrels sometimes move by the thousands across the country. They have no place to go, but they all move in the same direction and nothing seems to stop them. When they come to rivers and lakes, they walk in and start swimming. Naturalists, a long time ago, told of millions of squirrels that moved in this way.

In 1968, as autumn approached, the squirrels moved again. Suddenly the woods of nine states, from New York to Alabama, were alive with traveling squirrels. Many drowned. Others were killed on highways. Biologists estimated that year that in those nine states eighty million squirrels left their homes.

Any gray squirrel that has its choice of a place to live would probably choose a hollow tree. But often there are not enough hollow trees to go around, and the squirrel must build itself a leaf nest in the treetops. When the leaves are off the trees in winter, these squirrel nests are easily seen against the sky.

The nests are made of leaves which the squirrel cuts during the late summer and carries to the place it has chosen for its home. Squirrels that live in hollow trees also carry leaves into their homes for a bed. I have watched the old mother squirrel carry new bed covers into her home in the wild cherry tree. One day she came to the door of her den carrying a long, leafy branch crossways in her mouth. She tried to walk through her doorway. She pushed, but the twig would not bend and let her through. She stopped. Then she turned the twig and poked one end of it through the door and disappeared with her mouthful of leaves.

Young gray squirrels sometimes do a poor job of nest building. One carried leaves to the very top of an oak tree, but instead of putting the nest in the strong forks near the trunk, it began building far out on the ends of the branches. The nest was a ball of leaves and twigs. Through the fall the young squirrel occasionally carried more building materials to it. But in December a wind storm blew the nest apart. We never knew where the squirrel moved, but we hoped it chose a better place for its new nest.

These leafy homes are usually snugly lined with a bed made of the inner bark of trees cut into fine threads. These are packed together into a soft, round bowl big enough to hold a squirrel.

Some nests make a home for several squirrels. In winter the old mother squirrel shares her cherry tree with other squirrels, usually

An adult gray squirrel peeks out from its nest, a cavity originally made by a woodpecker.

her young ones, whom she may keep with her until a new litter is due. Through the winter they snuggle close together in the nest for warmth. There may sometimes be more than one adult squirrel in the same nest.

Squirrels' homes also become homes for insects. The insects eat the leaves in the nest and the squirrels must repair their homes. There are also tiny pests that live in the squirrel's fur coat. One of these pests is a little eight-legged mite that causes mange, a skin disease which causes the squirrel's fur to fall out. One winter several squirrels living in our woods lost most of the fur in their tails. The tails, once bushy and beautiful, became almost naked. When the squirrels flicked their tails not much happened. These tails no longer helped them keep their balance while running along the limbs. The tails were no longer blankets to help insulate the squirrels against the cold nights. This can be serious to a squirrel. But if they live through the winter, they can grow new coats of hair.

This squirrel is probably attempting to remove a parasite from its fur.

On almost any winter day the squirrels will be outdoors. They come down from their treetops and hop around on the snow, sniffing for buried nuts. Or they sit in the sun with their backs to the wind.

But when a storm sweeps across the land, the squirrels may go indoors and stay for two or three days. The gray squirrels never hibernate. But they may curl up and spend a lot of time sleeping and waiting for the weather to get better.

By late winter the gray squirrels have come to their breeding season. The old females, and also the young ones born the year before, are ready for mating. They may have two litters of young in a year, with the first mating coming perhaps in February and the second in June.

Forty days after the mating the young are born. Sometimes there may be three or sometimes five, but usually there are four of them. The gray squirrel when first born is tiny and helpless. It weighs only about half an ounce, has no fur to protect it from the cold, and must be kept warm with heat from the mother's body. Its eyes are sealed and its ears are closed. Its head looks too big for its little body and so do its four big feet.

At first the baby squirrel grows slowly. Its ears do not open until it is twenty-eight days old, and its eyes are sealed tightly until it is thirty-two days old. Before the little squirrel's eyes open, the first soft hair appears on its body. Gradually the covering of hair thickens and when the young squirrel is two months old it is about half the size of its parents and looks like a little copy of them with its long bushy tail.

Mother squirrels will attack enemies to protect their nests and have been known to leap onto people and scratch and bite them. If the young are threatened, she may move her entire family to a new location. This is hard work for her. She must carry the young, helpless squirrels one at a time from the old nest to the new one. To do this she turns the baby over and gets a firm grip on its chest, and then takes it for a long bumpy ride out into the cold world.

Because they live in the trees, gray squirrels do not face as many hazards as the rabbits and other wild creatures that must live at ground level. Foxes or dogs can seldom get to them. Hawks sometimes pick the unwary squirrel from its treetop perch. The gray squirrel that stays out too late in the evening twilight or leaves its den in the first light of morning may become a meal for the barred owl or the great-horned owl. Raccoons will sometimes

This curious young gray squirrel has just recently left its nest.

take the young squirrels from the nest when the mother squirrel is off gathering food. The slow-moving opossum will do the same if it can.

Snakes are a special enemy of young squirrels. One day a black rat snake about four feet long was climbing the old cherry tree straight up toward the old mother squirrel's home. A pair of blue-jays that lives in the woods the year around set up a clamor that brought me to the window to watch.

The old squirrel came out of the top of a nearby oak tree. She

A young gray squirrel learning to climb.

ran over and took a position on a limb above her den and sat there scolding the snake. She chattered and barked and twitched her tail while the bluejays flew close to the reptile and screeched at it.

Slowly the snake worked its way to the entrance of the old squirrel's den. But it had come at a time when there were no young in the tree. They were well grown and I could see at least two of them looking down on the visiting snake from a safe distance in another tree.

Others have seen gray squirrels leap right onto snakes that came near their nests. One squirrel grabbed a long black snake by the head and shook the reptile loose from the tree, then dropped it to the ground. Shortly after the snake hit the ground, the angry squirrel was there also. It had raced down the tree and once more grabbed the snake and gave it another good shaking before rushing back up into the tree.

But often the snakes win. Large black snakes have been known to swallow half-grown gray squirrels.

The gray squirrel that escapes its enemies may live to be ten or twelve years old. Most of them you see dashing about in the treetops, however, are not yet five, and any one living beyond its sixth birthday is an old squirrel.

Most gray squirrels still live in the woods. For neighbors they have noisy bluejays, great-horned owls that call in the night, and red-bellied woodpeckers that wake them up in the morning knocking on their trees. But some of these country squirrels have moved to town, where they have people and pigeons and dogs for neighbors.

Squirrels in town can get into a lot of trouble. They are curious about everything they find, poking their heads into dark places searching for new homes, or chewing on strange things, soft or hard. In Ohio a gray squirrel once chewed through the wire of a television antenna. The picture went off. Then the people next door reported that their television went off also. And after repair-men came and fixed the wires, the squirrels came back and chewed some more.

A big coal company in Pennsylvania once had a problem because squirrels would make the entire coal mine close down. Steel towers higher than the trees held up big electric lines. Through these lines ran 11,000 volts of electricity to keep the mine machinery running. Gray squirrels often played on the towers, a dangerous place for them. Sometimes a squirrel's body would cause a short in the wiring. Sparks would flash; wires would hum and crackle and smoke. Everything jerked to a stop, including the squirrel, which fell dead beneath the tower. The miners would walk out of the deep mine and go home for the day, while electricians repaired the damage.

Telephone companies worry about squirrels too. Squirrels in one community learned to drop out of their trees onto the telephone lines, where they quietly sat sharpening their teeth on the covering of the wires. The first time it rained, water seeped into the wires and short-circuited them, and telephones went dead all over the neighborhood. This has happened may times in many places, and unhappy repair crews have to run around behind the squirrels fixing the lines.

Squirrels crossing the street sometimes get automobile drivers into trouble. A woman in Wisconsin saw a gray squirrel dash out of a yard and run in front of her car. Quickly she swerved to the left. She missed the squirrel. But her car ran up into a driveway, crashed into another automobile, then banged into the house. While the squirrel spent the following days hunting nuts in the trees, the woman that spared its life spent a few days in the hospital. She also had to pay the garage to take all the dents out of her car.

Some city squirrels have solved this traffic problem by running along overhead utility lines stretched across the street. Trees grow-

A gray squirrel searching for an escape from a garage.

ing out over quiet old streets also make a bridge for squirrels. They can cross through the branches and cause no trouble at all. In New York City one naturalist insists that a squirrel he knows always waits for the green light before crossing Fifth Avenue to eat where the pigeons are fed. Green light or red, it seems a risky business, especially for someone no taller than a squirrel.

In Pennsylvania a gray squirrel ran beneath a parked automobile, then crawled up above the engine, where it hid under the hood. The car owner saw the squirrel go under the car and observed that it did not come out, but he forgot to mention it. His brother came out some hours later and drove to the nearby service station. "Check under the hood, sir?"

"Please."

The attendant lifted the hood and out leaped a full-grown gray squirrel that began running around the gas pumps. Then, as soon as the hood was slammed shut, the squirrel crawled back up inside the car, where it stayed for the ride home. That evening it slipped out and ran off into the woods and never came back for another ride.

A Missouri farmer said squirrels were following him down the rows when he planted corn. As fast as he could put the yellow grains in the soft earth, the hungry squirrels would dig them out and eat them. He finally had to scatter a couple of bushels of corn along the edges of his field for the squirrels so they would leave the seed alone long enough for it to grow.

Once they get inside a house, squirrels can cause real trouble. They occasionally find a way into an attic where is is dry and warm. One way into the house for squirrels is down the chimney. A woman called the conservation officer about a squirrel that came in this way. "It jumped out of the fireplace," she said, "and started helping itself to nuts and Christmas cookies."

Meanwhile, a woman in Indiana called the state conservation office. "I've been chasing a squirrel around my house for hours," she cried, "trying to catch it. Now I've got it cornered in the bathroom. But I don't know what to do next." The conservation officer arrived, carrying a trout landing net. The squirrel was too tired to run much more, and the officer quickly scooped it into the net, took it to the woods, and turned it free.

Another squirrel, preparing for the winter, moved into a storage shed which seemed well stocked with just what it needed. The owner had stored corn in one half of the shed; in the other half he had stacked some insulation that he intended to use on his home. The squirrel cut up enough of the insulating material to make itself a cozy nest right in the middle of the corn pile. There it stayed snug and warm and well fed through the winter.

Many years ago people in England learned about the gray squirrels of North America. How nice it must be, they thought, to have these sleek little acrobats leaping like magic about the tree-tops. They already had a squirrel of their own, but they wanted the gray squirrel anyhow. They wanted it so badly that cages of gray squirrels were soon being stowed aboard ships and sent to England, where the squirrels were turned free in the forests.

These foreign gray squirrels seemed to like their new land. They were at home in the maples, oaks, and elms, and they began to spread. This was all right until the gray squirrels began stripping bark from valuable trees. But it was too late for the English people to change their minds. The gray rascals continued to spread until they are now found over large sections of the British Isles.

These American gray squirrels have also been turned free in South Africa and Australia. Almost everywhere that it has been introduced, the gray squirrel has been called a pest and people wished they had left it at home.

Sometimes gray squirrels are not gray at all. In some northern states there are many black squirrels. This is a color phase of the gray squirrel, and they have the same scientific name, *Sciurus carolinensis*. Sometimes a female gray squirrel will have both gray and black young in the same litter.

Other gray squirrels are white. Some of these have no color pigment, and they have the red eyes of the pure albino. But others have white coats and dark eyes. In Olney, Illinois, there are white squirrels all over town. People of Olney are very proud of the white squirrels that climb in their trees and run across their lawns. They call their city the "White Squirrel Town."

Their squirrels would be gray like other gray squirrels if it had not been for a saloon keeper and his unusual idea back in 1902. He bought a pair of fancy squirrels—one was pure white, the other cream-colored. For a while he had the two blond squirrels in the window of his saloon. People passing by stopped and watched the squirrels; never before had they seen such animals.

But the saloon keeper was told that he was not allowed to keep squirrels in captivity, so he took them to the park and turned them loose. They lived in the park, and when they mated, their young ones were pure white. The next year more white squirrels were born in Olney, and eventually the town had only white squirrels. There were more than a thousand of these animals in Olney.

In the "White Squirrel Town," laws have been passed to keep people from harming the animals. White squirrels that want to cross a street have the right-of-way, and automobiles and trucks and bicycles must stop for them. Any person convicted of harming a white squirrel in Olney, or of taking one out of town, is fined $25. All in all, life in Olney has been good for white squirrels.

Gray squirrels are sometimes kept by people who want them for pets. The people may not know, at least not at first, that squirrels tear up furniture and curtains, and get into all kinds of food around a house. Most wild animals do not make good pets. They are born to run wild. Locked up in pens they come to depend on people for their food and safety. And too often people do not know how such an animal should be fed or what care it should be given. Besides, it is usually against the law to keep wild animals, although some people have been given special permission to keep squirrels.

A friend of mine and his wife once raised two little gray squirrels, a story that began with a tragedy. Three days after the squirrels were born, one day in August, dark clouds moved out of the west. The storm winds blew, thunder roared, and lightning flashed in the sky, and the top of the oak tree swayed back and forth. Then the rain stopped, and soon the mother slipped out of the nest. Perhaps she was a young female that had never before built a leaf nest, and it may have been poorly constructed. Cold rain may have dripped through the leaves against the skin of one of the babies. They began moving in their nest, which was forty feet above the ground.

Two baby squirrels slipped over the edge and turned over and over in the air as they plunged toward the ground. They landed on a thick soft grass in the front yard of my friend's home.

If a cat had come by at that moment, the two baby squirrels, not much bigger than mice, would be gone. Or a dog might have taken them, or even a bird could have carried them off. If it had happened in the deep forest instead of a front yard, they would surely have died, unless the young mother heard their squeaks and came and carried them quickly back to the nest.

But when the woman living in the house came out to see what damage the storm might have done to her trees and flowers, she heard the little squirrels squeaking beneath the oak tree. She picked them up, carried them into the house, and wrapped them in a warm blanket.

There was no way to put them back in their damaged treetop nest, so the woman and her husband became the new parents of two little squirrels. They named one Frisky and the other Whiskers. Every four hours they fed them milk with an eye dropper. They set their alarm clock and got up in the middle of the night to give Frisky and Whiskers their milk. The squirrels did well, but the man and his wife were sometimes very tired in the morning.

Their baby gray squirrels grew stronger every day and a little

Frisky gets fed some milk from an eye dropper.

A friendly terrier checks on Frisky and Whiskers.

bit bigger. When they opened their eyes for the first time, they did not see what most young gray squirrels see. Instead of gray squirrels for parents, they knew only a man and a woman who fed them and petted them.

By the time their eyes were first opening, it was easy to tell the squirrels apart. Frisky was always active. He investigated every corner of the basket in which they lived. He was always ready to eat. His brother, Whiskers, was slower and calmer.

They were kept warm with an electric blanket, and they grew strong on cow's milk fed from the eye dropper. When they were old enough to see, they began eating little bits of hard-boiled egg.

This family also had a little black fox terrier that helped take care of the squirrels. When Frisky or Whiskers were out on the floor, the dog would stay nearby and protect them from danger. Sometimes it would lie down and let the young gray squirrels crawl over it and play. The dog was very happy—it had never had pets of its own before.

But the people wanted to turn the squirrels free as soon as they were old enough to take care of themselves.

Hickory trees stood thick in the back yard. These trees were already the home for many gray squirrels, and there were no hollow limbs left vacant. It was already late in the fall and the young squirrels had never before built a leaf nest to shelter them in winter, so the man began building a squirrel nest box.

Nearly anyone can build a nest box for gray squirrels. An old nail keg will do well if it has a hole in the side near the top big enough for squirrels and is placed high in a tree. Or a squirrel box can be made of wood. It should be 1½ feet high and 7½ inches square, with an entrance near the top that measures 3 by 4 inches. These boxes are often made by people who want more wild squirrels around their property.

Whiskers and Frisky learning to climb during one of their first outdoor experiences.

The box made for Frisky and Whiskers was big and tightly constructed so the wind could not whistle through. It was placed in the tree behind the house. But the only home the squirrels knew was the basket where they first opened their eyes, and at first Frisky and Whiskers jumped out of the new box and followed the woman back to the house. They hated dead leaves in their nest—they much preferred a towel and an electric blanket.

But they did like climbing, and they spent much time those first

SQUIRRELS

days racing through trees. They were not afraid of the highest places. They played tag on tiny limbs that bent and rocked with their weight. And when they grew tired of playing games in the trees, they would stop and rest. More and more they used the new box that had been built for them.

The squirrels soon began searching the trees for their own food. They knew about hickory nuts because they had been given some to chew on while still living in a basket in the house. When they discovered a hickory nut in the yard, they would grab it in their mouth and dash for the nearest tree. Then they would climb to a limb and sit there with their backs against the trunk of the tree while chewing through the tough shell to get to the kernels inside.

But when they could find no food of their own, they returned to the back door of the house where they had once lived. They scratched around the door and the door opened. Then the woman leaned down and handed them hickory nuts and peanuts and called them Whiskers and Frisky.

She knew, however, that gray squirrels do not belong in houses. They are at home in the forest or in the trees at the city park, where they do not have to depend on people for everything. They can be independent, the way the old mother squirrel in our back yard is independent. Nobody tells her when to come or go. She does as she likes the year around. She races through the trees like a gray demon streaking along the limbs. Or she stretches out on a limb near her home and rests contentedly in the sun. Usually she sleeps late in the morning and comes out for breakfast whenever the spirit moves her. This is the independent life of the gray squirrel.

Chapter three

~~~~~~~~~~~~~~~~~~~~~~~~~~~~~~~~~~

SQUIRRELS WITH TASSELS ON THEIR EARS

If you should travel to the Grand Canyon in the northern part of Arizona, watch for the squirrels. They have fancy tassels on their ears and special colors as well.

These tree squirrels are found on both the north side of the canyon and the south side. They measure a foot long, and their bodies are big and chunky. Besides, they have tails about eight or nine inches long which gives them a total length of eighteen to twenty inches. You will have no problem recognizing them. When their fur is in prime shape, they have long, blackish tufts of hair sticking up from the points of their ears, and they have fancier colors than most squirrels.

These squirrels do not have the choice of foods enjoyed by their cousins living in the forests of the eastern states. They do not know what a hickory nut tastes like. Instead they feed mostly on pine trees. Sometimes they eat the seeds of the ponderosa pine; but usually they have to make a meal of the inner bark, or cambium layer.

The tassel-eared squirrel has a special method of harvesting this inner bark. It edges cautiously out toward the thin, swaying tip of a branch. Then it nips off the end and lets the pine needles fall to the ground. This is not the part it is after. Instead, it wants a

This Kaibab squirrel, one of the most beautiful of North American squirrels, was photographed while feeding on a snag on the north rim of the Grand Canyon, the only place it is found.

section of the branch right behind the tip. It snips off about six inches of this twig with its sharp teeth, then carries it back to a safer and more comfortable place in the tree to have its lunch. Sitting up in the approved squirrel position, the big, colorful animal with the tassel ears begins stripping the outer bark from the twig so it can get to the soft, white cambium layer beneath it.

Unlike many squirrels, the tassel-eared squirrels do not store large quantities of food. Sometimes they hide away modest stores of foods that will last into the winter. Perhaps they do not find it necessary to save up for winter, because all year they have a good supply of pine twigs available. During the winter they may sleep for several days at a time and not need to eat. In addition to the cambium layer, however, they will eat nuts, fruits, and birds' eggs if they can find them.

For shelter the tassel-eared squirrels usually build nests of pine twigs with the needles still on them. They weave the twigs together, arrange the pine needles, and line the inside tightly with grass and bark. Even in the coldest winter their nests protect them from the winds that blow across the mountains. In these nests the females have their litters of three or four young ones, usually in early April.

There is a strange story in the history of these tassel-eared squirrels. For millions of years erosion cut the Grand Canyon deeper and deeper. Finally the squirrels on either side could no longer travel beyond the edge of the mile-deep valley. That giant canyon had cut right through the tassel-eared squirrel's range and isolated those that lived on the north side from the squirrels on the south rim.

These northern tassel-eared squirrels live nowhere else in the world. Their home is in the Kaibab National Forest and the Grand Canyon National Park. The Kaibab Plateau is seventy miles long and about thirty miles wide, and these tassel-eared squirrels have never spread out beyond the Kaibab Plateau. To their west, north, and east lies only dry country without trees. To their south lies the Grand Canyon. They are locked into their range.

Over the centuries they began to develop colors different from those of their southern cousins. Mammologists still debate whether the two kinds of tassel-eared squirrels are separate species. Some say they are, others maintain they are only races of the same species. Perhaps they are still evolving into different species.

They are easily told apart. The group in the high country on the north side of the Grand Canyon, known as Kaibab squirrels, have fancy tails that are all white and underparts that are black. The squirrels to the south of the canyon are known as Abert's squirrels. Their tails are white below, but gray on the upper surface with a broad border of white hairs. They have white underparts. The Abert's squirrel also has a reddish brown stripe running down its back and a shorter blackish stripe on either side. These stripes are missing in the blackish Kaibab squirrel.

People are worried about the Kaibab squirrels living north of the Grand Canyon, for there are only a few thousand left. Their habitat may no longer be as good for them as it once was. Automobiles frequently run over them on the forest highways. Perhaps they suffer from disease. Whatever the reasons, the Kaibab squirrel is on the federal government's official list of threatened animals. They cannot be legally hunted. The forest and park lands where they live in the Ponderosa pines are considered a sanctuary, the only place in the world for these squirrels with the strange tasseled ears and beautiful white tails.

This red squirrel has chosen an elevated platform on which to eat.

Chapter four

~~~~~~~~~~~~~~~~~~~~~~~~~~~~~~~~

RED SQUIRRELS

Red squirrels are tattletales. They sit up in the green treetops, chattering and gabbling back and forth and telling on anyone who might be walking through the woods. They scold in loud, shrill voices. And when one starts, another one, some distance away, picks up the word and begins scolding also.

Not only are they the most talkative squirrels in the forest, they are also the smallest of the tree-climbing squirrels that normally come out in daytime. The red squirrel is about half the size of a gray squirrel, perhaps twelve-and-a-half inches long including its tail, and weighing no more than five-and-a-half ounces.

In addition to its small size and saucy manner, the red squirrel can be told by its generally reddish coat and pointed ears.

This little gossip lives over a wide range of North American forest. It is found across Alaska and Canada to the Atlantic Ocean, then southward into the northern states and down the mountain ranges of the Appalachians and Rockies. In the ever-green forests of the Pacific Northwest and southward into the mountains of California lives a cousin of the red squirrel, some-what darker in color, but equally noisy in the forest. This little squirrel is the chickaree. Some people also call the red squirrel by this name.

The red squirrel seems to want the best of both worlds. It is often seen down on the ground, although most of its time is spent in the trees. It dashes nimbly along the smaller limbs as if there is no fear in its heart. But it does not hesitate to come down on the ground, where it seems more at home than either the gray or fox squirrel. Often it runs down one tree, dashes a short distance across the ground, then races back up another tree.

In addition, it feeds on the ground much of the time. Unlike other tree squirrels, the red squirrel does not usually bury its winter food items one at a time in the ground. Instead it may bring all these good things together in one place where every day it can survey its wealth of pine cones and enjoy its meals in the same place. It has been known to store as much as two quarts of hickory nuts in one place. This is known as its midden pile, and the hungry red squirrel sits in the midst of this collection and eats while scattering shells and hulls all around. The red squirrel may have several such midden piles where it stores food.

The red squirrel's foods are mostly pine cones and nuts when these are available. Many a tree owes its start in life to a red squirrel that buried a seed and then failed to find it. These squirrels also collect mushrooms that they sometimes leave to dry for winter food.

A large part of its spring and summer foods may consist of twigs and buds. It is also accused often of being a nest robber preying on the birds in its community. Although this reputation seems to be deserved, it is likely that not all red squirrels have equal opportunities to rob nests.

For a home the red squirrel usually favors vacated woodpecker holes. Here the female red squirrel throws out the bird's nest and builds her own. It makes a fine place to have her young. Flying squirrels sometimes compete with red squirrels for these choice living quarters.

In addition the red squirrel may build bulky leaf nests in the trees nearby. This still may not offer enough variety, so the red squirrel may dig itself another dwelling beneath a fallen log or in a rock pile, maybe with several short tunnels into which the little squirrel can vanish.

The breeding season comes late in winter and the young red squirrels are born in April, May, and June. There are three to six in each litter and they are about four-and-a-half inches long, hairless, blind, and helpless. Within about a month, however, they have acquired enough hair to resemble their parents, and a few weeks later they will be out there in the trees learning how to be successful red squirrels, chattering at everything they see in the woods.

A fox squirrel in a red oak tree.

Chapter five

FOX SQUIRRELS

Biggest of all the tree squirrels are the fox squirrels. Some of them are two feet long if you measure their long hairy tails.

There are three color phases of fox squirrels. Some wear rusty, reddish-colored coats. Others are more gray. The third kind scientists call "melanistic," all black.

Perhaps at no time were fox squirrels ever as common as the smaller gray squirrels. Fox squirrels live throughout the eastern part of the United States and as far west as North Dakota and south into Texas.

Fox squirrels have been taken West and turned free in parks and on college campuses. Sometimes they learn that people want to feed them peanuts; such squirrels may become so tame they come up to eat from a person's hand.

These are squirrels of the big trees. They seem at home in the neat open woods where there is not a lot of brush. Pasture fields with large nut trees standing in them are fox squirrel country. For a den tree this squirrel usually selects one with a view; from its lofty palace it can look out and see the surrounding woods.

Sometimes the fox squirrel does not even run back up into its tree if a predator chases it. Instead it dashes along on the ground, running at about eleven miles an hour, passing tree after tree. Finally it comes to its own tree, scurries up the side of it and runs around to the far side. There the fox squirrel clings silently to the bark, hiding and waiting to see what will happen.

Hollow tree dens are the fox squirrels' first choice for a home. If the hollow trees are near water, a pair of wood ducks may try to chase the squirrels away. Fox squirrels may also try to chase the wood ducks out. Who wins depends on who got there first, because the one already in possession can usually defend its property.

But the number of hollow tree dens available for squirrels may be limited. When there is none to be had, the fox squirrel builds itself a nest of leaves, often in the strong forks of a large tree. It may build different kinds of leaf nests for different uses. For a summer nest, when the weather is nice, the fox squirrel may build a flimsy shelter, one the cooling breezes can blow through. Such a nest, sometimes called a shade, may take only half an hour of gathering and carrying leaves and twigs; and the nest may last only a few weeks.

When food is abundant, the squirrel may build a temporary combination eating and sleeping platform low in the tree. This is convenient because the squirrel does not have to go far to find a place to eat the food it gathers. If the fox squirrel has a nut in its mouth, instead of climbing to the regular den in the treetop, it can run up to the feeding platform for its snack. Then if it gets tired, which the fox squirrel seems to do often, it can settle down for a nap.

But when the fox squirrel must build its winter leaf nest, it does a careful job. Twigs, complete with leaves, are woven together to form the bulky outer shell. Then, inside, the squirrel plasters numerous layers of leaves around the wall, floor, and ceiling. These form a shelter that will keep out the rain and wind and let the

A fox squirrel approaching its leaf nest.

skilled builder keep warm and snug even in a storm. This leaf house may even have a self-closing door, made of leaves or bark, to cover the entrance.

Sometimes the fox squirrel allows other wild neighbors to build the foundation for its home. Crows do an excellent job—their abandoned nest may become the base for the fox squirrel's leaf house. Other times the fox squirrel may be fortunate enough to find a flicker house which some bird lover has nailed high up in a tree.

This squirrel needs a good solid winter home because it spends a lot of time there. It sleeps when there is nothing else to do; and in winter, during stormy weather, it may curl up in its treetop nest and sleep for several days.

Food for this large squirrel includes the seeds and nuts of almost any tree within its one-to-two-acre territory. Oak, hickory, beech, walnut, butternut, black cherry, elm, basswood, maple, ash, and coniferous trees all provide food that helps fatten the fox squirrel and see it through the long winters.

Farmers may sometimes tell you that fox squirrels also like tender, ripening corn better than all other kinds of foods. They may be right, because when the corn begins to ripen, and there are tassels on the tops of the plants, the fox squirrels come down from their trees to help the farmer with the corn harvest. When there is corn they may neglect all their natural foods and even neglect for several days to store food for the winter.

Like its gray cousin, the fox squirrel buries food for winter. One fox squirrel may bury thousands of nuts during the autumn months. Most of those found again are located by the squirrel's sharp sense of smell. Because the sense of smell is better when there is dampness, the squirrel may do far better at recovering these nuts if it buries them in moist soil. But no matter what type of soil it uses for its hiding grounds, there will likely be some left over to sprout in spring and perhaps grow into new nut trees.

For the fox squirrel the breeding season arrives in January, through most of its range. After forty-five days the mated female gives birth to her litter of two to five young, probably three. These babies are hairless and helpless, blind and deaf. For forty days their eyes will remain sealed.

By the time they are six weeks old, however, they look much like their parents, except that they are smaller. Then these young fox squirrels begin to come from their home and explore the big world outdoors. They stay with their mother for another month.

The Delmarva Peninsula fox squirrel is now
in danger of extinction.

By this time they have gained in size and weight, and now they
must go searching for homes of their own.

One of the most beautiful of all the races of fox squirrels is
found along the east coast of the United States on the Delmarva
Peninsula, which is part of the three states of Delaware, Virginia,
and Maryland. These Delmarva Peninsula fox squirrels are big,
light-gray-colored squirrels. They are in serious trouble because
forests have been cut and burned until there are not many Delmarva Peninsula fox squirrels left. This is why the United States
Government has this squirrel's name on its long list of wild animals that are in danger of extinction.

Chapter six

~~~~~~~~~~~~~~~~~~~~~~~~~~~

FLYING SQUIRRELS

There lives in our woods a little squirrel that we almost never see because he does not often come out in daylight. But while the gray squirrels and the chipmunks are sleeping through the dark hours, this little cousin is out enjoying the night life. It has found a way of traveling that other squirrels refuse to try—it goes by air.

I know an old oak tree where a flying squirrel lives sixty feet above the ground. The cavity originally belonged to a woodpecker family, but flying squirrels like these woodpecker holes and often appropriate them for themselves. The entrance is about the right size, the depth is fine, and the hollowed-out room is snug. All the little squirrel has to do is toss out some of the old wood chips used as bedding by the woodpecker, and carry in materials for its own nest. The flying squirrel uses shredded strips of fine underbark from trees along with bits of lichens to make a soft warm mattress.

Sometimes you can catch a nighttime glimpse of the flying squirrels as they visit the bird feeder on pleasant evenings. They glide down out of the trees and land with a little thump on the feeder. Soon all their cousins have also arrived for the feast.

At other times you may hear them in the dark of the night woods. If they are feeding on nuts, you hear them cutting the

Flying squirrels come at night to eat sunflower seeds.

shells with their long, sharp incisors and letting the fragments drop down through the leaves. Or you hear them chattering back and forth to each other. And if you flash your light into the trees, it may catch the reddish-orange reflection of the flying squirrel's eyes.

The body of an adult flying squirrel is only about six inches long. Add the length of the tail and it comes to nine or ten inches. Those that live in the northern forests of Canada and the high mountain ranges of the United States are slightly larger.

Scientists divide the North American flying squirrels into two species, the northern and southern. They are difficult to tell apart even if you have them in your hand. Like most squirrels, they are plain colored. Their bodies, except for the white underparts, are olive brown in color. The difference is found in the amount of white on the hair of the belly. Southern flying squirrels have hair on their underside that is white all the way to its base. Its northern cousin has white belly fur too, but the hairs become gray near their base.

Traveling in darkness, as it does, the flying squirrel needs large eyes. Its sight is excellent. It also has large ears and hears well the sounds of the night world around it.

The flying squirrel has equipment other squirrels do not possess. A loose, fur-covered membrane called the patagium stretches from the wrist on its front legs to the ankle. When it "flies" these membrances stretch out and turn the little squirrel's body into a parachute. When it is not sailing off on the breezes, the flying squirrel's "wings" fold back out of the way. There is a small spur sticking out from its front legs which helps it stretch the skin out still more, increasing the surface supporting it against the air.

This seems to be all the flying squirrel needs to help it in its wild free leaps through the night. Actually flying squirrels do not really fly; they glide instead. When the little squirrel reaches a respectable elevation in a tree and wants to be in a nearby tree, it simply leaps out into the black night. Then it follows a long, curving trail down toward the base of another tree. At the last moment before its landing, the squirrel flicks its flat tail upward. This acts as a brake and also tips its body so it can land flat against the tree and its feet can touch the bark. The soft pads on the squirrel's feet help absorb the shock. The instant it lands, it is likely to dash around to the far side of the tree, in case the silent-flying owl is on the flying squirrel's trail.

As it glides through the night, the squirrel can even change courses if it becomes necessary to avoid a limb or escape an owl. The flying squirrel can turn at a nearly ninety-degree angle by moving its feet or using its tail as a rudder.

This travel plan gives the flying squirrel great freedom. In a single leap it sometimes glides for 150 feet, although most leaps are shorter. Then it runs up the tree on which it lands and may leap out again and move on to tree after tree.

Flying squirrels are experts at making soft landings; they touch down like a feather. These squirrels are equipped with air brakes. If they want to slow down they can maneuver against the air until they almost stall. Some years ago, as Victor H. Cahalane has written in his book *Mammals Of North America*, a group of students kept a family of pet flying squirrels with which they played a special game. They began tossing one of the squirrels across the room to each other. They found that each time they tossed it, the squirrel made a soft landing against the squirrel catcher. It did not seem to matter how hard they threw the little squirrel—the landing was always the same beautiful, controlled maneuver. According to the students, even the squirrels did not seem to mind being used in this game of toss. It does, however, seem to be risky treatment for a creature as gentle and fragile as a flying squirrel.

Flying squirrels get along well together during the winter

months, when they spend most of their nights, as well as their days, curled up in their warm nests soundly asleep. There may be a dozen or more flying squirrels in the same nest in winter, all curled up and packed together into one warm ball of fur. One winter day many years ago near Beaver Dam, Wisconsin, W. E. Snyder found a nest of flying squirrels holding a slumber party in a hollow burr oak tree. He gently picked the ball of squirrels apart and counted them—there were twenty-two flying squirrels crowded into the one den!

But as spring awakens the woodland community again, the squirrels come to life. Each is likely to go back to its own home again because the most important time of the year is just ahead. There are new families of flying squirrels to be raised.

The mating season comes in late winter and the young are born during March or April, forty days after the parents have mated. Three or four young are the usual number. At birth five of them together weigh about an ounce.

The female is an excellent and devoted mother. She nurses her new young about once an hour, and within one week after birth they have doubled their weight. When they are six weeks old, they weigh ten times what they weighed at birth. The little flying squirrels, born naked and blind, begin to show a covering of thin hair at two weeks, and their eyes are open when they are a month old. A month later they are fully furred and weigh perhaps two-thirds as much as the mother. When they are six weeks old, the young ones begin to come out of the den and gather some of their own food.

When her family is in danger, the mother will quickly move them to a new home if one is to be found. How does she get there while carrying a baby? She flies, of course. She turns the little one over and grasps its underside in her mouth. Then she runs up the tree, somehow managing not to scrape and crush her young one

A young flying squirrel.

against the bark. When she has reached her launching pad, far up in the tree, she gathers her strength and leaps out into the open air. In this way she moves her family to a new tree home, ferrying the youngsters one by one until all are in their new quarters. Squirrels cannot count. After the last young squirrel is moved, the mother makes a final trip to the nest and searches thoroughly to see if she has missed anyone.

One woodsman felled a tree only to learn that it held a nest of young flying squirrels. He wondered what the frantic mother squirrel would do. He stood in one place and held the nest of babies in his hand. The female climbed his pants leg, took one baby, and ferried it to a nearby tree where she placed it in a vacant hole. Then she returned and took the others, showing no fear of the man and not hesitating until her task was complete.

There are many creatures that eat flying squirrels. They are doubtless taken on occasion by foxes and other predators that catch them on the ground where they are not very agile or quick moving. Cats are known to catch flying squirrels. Tree-climbing snakes sometimes enter their dens and feed on the young or even the adults if they can corner them.

But perhaps the owls with which the flying squirrels share the night are their most serious enemy. Owls fly on noiseless wings. They have big eyes to tell them what moves in the darkness. And owls must eat too.

In addition, men have cut the trees in which the flying squirrels live and from which they obtain the foods they need. Forest fires, often set by careless people, also destroy the woods and kill the creatures caught in their dens.

Favorite foods of the flying squirrel include beechnuts, hickory nuts, and acorns. This little squirrel has a special way of cutting a nut that reveals its presence to naturalists. It opens a hickory nut by cutting a circular or oval hole in one side. Fox and gray squirrels cut the nut all apart, scattering pieces of the shell over the forest floor. Deer mice, unlike the flying squirrel, make two openings in the shell.

In spring when their supplies of nuts run low, the flying squirrels eat the newly developing buds and flowers of trees and shrubs. They sometimes follow yellow-bellied sapsuckers and lap up the sap oozing from new woodpecker holes. They are especially

A flying squirrel and its hickory nut.

fond of maple sap, and farmers who hang open buckets on maple trees to collect the sap in late winter sometimes find the little gliding squirrels drowned in the sweet fluids.

Large insects are choice tablefare, and June beetles and the large-bodied moths that inhabit the night are big game for the flying squirrel. One boy who kept a pet flying squirrel glanced at the window one night to see a big cecropia moth, attracted to the light, fluttering against the outside of the glass. His pet flying squirrel saw it too and leaped at the window in an effort to catch the insect through the glass. The boy captured the moth and brought it in for his pet. The squirrel consumed it quickly, and afterward it was often given beetles and moths for its nighttime snacks.

The flying squirrel holds its food with its front feet while eating, then licks its paws and uses them to scrub its face afterward.

People like flying squirrels, for these are animals that seldom do much damage. Besides, they make fine pets and often seem perfectly contented to live with their human owners. The flying squirrels, however, may get into serious trouble if they move into the attic. When everyone else in the house is ready for bed, the flying squirrels upstairs are wide awake and full of energy. They scamper over the floor, and they may roll nuts on the attic floor, creating noise that disturbs the people downstairs.

People who keep flying squirrels for pets often carry them around in their pockets. Anyone who has kept a flying squirrel remembers it for its curiosity. One of my friends nearly lost his pet squirrel the day his mother had a large pan of plum jam on the kitchen stove. The squirrel, probably smelling the tantalizing odors, climbed a curtain on the far side of the room. From near the ceiling it launched itself in the direction of the stove. Its control and judgment were excellent, and it should have been proud of its pinpoint landing—it splashed down squarely in the middle of the pot. Flying squirrels are poor swimmers because the flap of skin with which they glide gets in their way in the water. Pet flying squirrels have landed in toilet bowls and been unable to escape. All that saved my friend's jam-covered pet was a big wooden spoon still in the pot, which the squirrel used to help it climb out. Next it hopped across the room, leaving purple stains behind it, and then climbed up the white curtain to sit near the ceiling, licking its fur. Nobody could get the squirrel's footprints off the curtain.

Some states have laws that protect flying squirrels, and anybody wanting to keep one as a pet should check with the local conservation officer first. The flying squirrel is quiet and clean in its habits. But it does not give up its nighttime ways. If allowed to roam freely, it may wait until you are asleep, then come gliding out of the night and thump down on your chest. You awaken to see two great dark eyes staring you in the face. In that instant before you come fully awake and remember that you are the owner of a pet flying squirrel, you may let out a scream that sends your pet looking for a place to hide.

Flying squirrels are fragile animals and easily injured. Those who handle them must remember never to squeeze or bump them, because rough action could kill a flying squirrel.

One man who kept a pet flying squirrel trained it to glide to him and land on his chest or hand. This squirrel has a remarkable ability to judge distance and depth. Before the pet squirrel would leap, it would move its head first to one side, then the other, then lift its head high and take a final look. When it leaped, it would be right on course and almost always land precisely on the spot the man patted with his hand.

When it has nothing else to do, the pet squirrel may spend most of the night carrying seeds or nuts from its food bowl and hiding them in its owner's coat pocket. One owner often carried his pet flying squirrel along on trips. "I could usually figure," he said, "that in one of my pockets I would find something for it to eat."

One naturalist friend of mine had a pet flying squirrel that traveled everywhere with him. The flying squirrel once went to the top of the Washington Monument with him. But it was not allowed to look out the window because it might get ideas about setting some kind of new distance record for its species.

Much of the time this little squirrel rode around sleeping in a little cardboard box on the front seat of the naturalist's car, and this led to a tragedy. One day while the naturalist was running some errands in town, his car was broken into by thieves. Among the things they stole was the little box on the front seat. When questioned by the police the naturalist listed among his lost items "one flying squirrel."

This brought a newspaper reporter asking about the kidnapped squirrel. What did the flying squirrel like to eat? "He especially liked peanuts and beer," the naturalist replied. The following morning the front page of the city paper carried a story pleading with those who had taken the flying squirrel. Would they please be sure to give it plenty of peanuts and beer. Perhaps they did. Nobody knows. The grieving owner never heard again of his little pet.

For all its appeal as a pet, the flying squirrel really belongs out of doors as a wild part of its ecosystem. It belongs in the woodlands, where it can glide about silently, filling the night with flitting shadows and always traveling by air in a way that nonflying squirrels would not dare.

Chapter seven

~~~~~~~~~~~~~~~~~~~~~~~~~~~~

CHIPMUNKS

On the first pleasant morning in late February I look out the back window and there by the edge of the woods is a chipmunk, the first one I have seen since autumn. He has come to the entrance of his burrow and found the woods flooded with warm sunlight. Most of the snow has melted. The air is nippy, but after his weeks of sleeping the little squirrel is eager to explore the outdoor world again.

He scampers around the brown leaves of the forest floor, poking his sharp little nose into dark places. He is always sniffing, for his nose tells him what is hidden beneath the leaves, under the edge of the log, or what the rock covers up.

He is nervous, as most chipmunks are. He stops often in his exploring and jerks his head up to survey the world around him. If there is no sign of hawk or cat or dog, he hurries back to his work.

Then the chipmunk leaps up onto a low, flat rock. From there he can jump to the top of a log that has fallen in the forest. He runs along the decaying tree trunk to a spot of bright sun falling on the log. The chipmunk stops in this spotlight like a comedian who has come to the center of the stage. The sun warms his fur and he sits there for nearly three minutes, rubbing his face with his paws and scratching his fur. This gives me a splendid opportunity to study the colors of his coat through my binoculars.

This is the eastern chipmunk. Several species live in the western part of North America. Western chipmunks are usually smaller and more gray than reddish. But the eastern species lives from southern Canada southward to the northwestern tip of Florida, then west to the eastern edge of Kansas, Nebraska, and Oklahoma. Within this range the chipmunk is well known to people because it often lives around homes and in parks.

As I adjust the binoculars and bring the chipmunk into sharp focus, I feel certain this one is a male because the males come from their winter homes two or three weeks before the females. The females are still down in their dark burrows sleeping and in no hurry to get up for the summer. The males, however, are restless. Hormones in their bodies are announcing the approach of the new mating season.

Sometimes a male goes courting the female before he is welcome and finds that she has her own harsh way of saying no. She may slash him around the head and neck with her long, sharp incisors—not just one nip and a slap, but an all-out fight. As soon as he can escape her fury, the rejected male dashes away to lick his wounds. He leaves her to her nasty ways and lets her sleep off her grumpy disposition for a few more weeks. These attacks by the females have been known to injure the males so badly they die; but this perhaps is rare.

Sitting on his log in the spot of sun, the chipmunk shows the fine colors and distinctive pattern of his fur coat. The gray squirrels, red squirrels, fox squirrels, and others may have to settle for plain outfits, but the chipmunk is a fashionable creature in the squirrel world. His upper parts are reddish-brown, or sometimes grayish toned. Running back from his shoulders to his rump is a fine assortment of stripes. Five of them are black stripes glistening in the sun. Just above the bottom stripe on each side is a broad band of white or cream-colored hair. There is a matching patch around the eye, while across this patch and the center of the eye runs a narrow, dark stripe. His rump is colored bright chestnut. The tail is a long, flat wand, dark above and lighter below. The colorful fur of his sides shades into a plain white on his belly. Twice a year the old hair is replaced by new, and the fur coat the chipmunk wears in winter is somewhat lighter in color than the one we see on him during the long summer days.

The chipmunk is a diminutive one in the world of squirrels, standing perhaps two inches tall at the shoulders and weighing between three and five ounces. Its total length, tail included, is eight to ten inches.

But what the chipmunk lacks in size it makes up in spirit. If you walk into its territory you may elicit a sharp "chuck" or "chip," and sometimes a loud call that starts out with a sharp "chip" but trills off into "chip-chur-r-r-r." Sometimes chipmunks seem to be calling each other or even setting up a chorus of high-pitched harmony.

The chipmunks do not need a large territory. Most of them probably live out their lives within half an acre. Sometimes, but not often, they fight about territory. Usually chipmunks get along rather well together.

This was noticed by John Burroughs, the famed naturalist of the Catskill Mountains and the Hudson Valley. "One March morning, after a light fall of snow," he recounts in his book *Riverby,* "I saw where one had come up out of his hole, which was in the side of our path to the vineyard, and after a moment's survey of the surroundings, had started off on his travels. I followed the track to see where he had gone. He had passed through my woodpile, then under the beehives, then around the study and under some spruces, and along the slope to the hole of a friend of his, about sixty yards from his own. Apparently he had gone in here, and then his friend had come forth with him, for there were two tracks leading from the doorway. I followed them to a third humble entrance, not far off, where the tracks were so numerous that I lost the trail."

These little squirrels live much of their lives in the darkness of their tunnels. Their security is underground, and if they are surprised while out in the open searching for food, they scamper off quickly to lose themselves in the safety of their cavelike homes.

Some animals that live underground seek out the dens and burrows of others, but the chipmunks prefer to design and fashion their own homes according to their needs and impulses. They are good at this work, often creating a series of tunnels that are long, twisting, and complex. The chipmunk's burrow, about two inches in diameter, may be thirty feet long. Far back toward the end of its tunnel, the chipmunk will dig out a bedroom about a foot high and a foot across. Then it may dig a spare bedroom as well. In addition, it will have a separate room to use as a toilet. There will also be two or three storage rooms into which it packs its winter food supplies.

The home of the chipmunk may be difficult to find, for the little squirrel does not announce its location in any way that might attract the attention of wild creatures that enjoy chipmunk meat. Anyone looking for chipmunks might think he could locate the burrow by just watching for the piles of dirt. Obviously all that dirt the chipmunks dig has to go somewhere. It is equally obvious that it has to go outside. If the chipmunk were to take a lesson from its big cousin the woodchuck, it could simply kick the dirt out the front door and leave it there in a pile advertising the entrance to its home. This, however, is exactly what the chipmunk avoids.

Straight down for three or four inches the chipmunk digs into the earth. Then it angles the tunnel off at about forty-five degrees until it is three feet or so below the surface. After this, the tunnel may turn in any direction, depending on the needs and whims of the little excavator.

As it digs the earth at the end of its tunnel, the little squirrel kicks it back. Then, when there is a good supply lying on the floor behind it, the chipmunk compresses itself into a ball and turns around to begin moving the dirt toward the entrance of the tunnel. This is slow work. The digging can go on year after year; as long as the chipmunk lives, it can be enlarging its home.

With its front paws and nose the chipmunk pushes the dirt to the entrance, then outside. Next it moves the dirt a good distance from the doorway, and then hurries back along the trail to move some more. There may be several such entrances to the tunnel before it is completed. Then, when its home is finished, the chipmunk has one final safety measure to install—it closes off the door through which it has carried the fresh earth and seals it completely.

John Burroughs was puzzled about this until the chipmunk helped him solve the mystery. "One day, when I paused before my little neighbor's mound of earth," he wrote in *Riverby*, "I saw that the hole was nearly stopped up, and while I was looking, the closure was completed from within. Loose earth was being shoved up from below and pressed into the opening; the movement of the soil could be seen. It flashed upon me at once that here was the key to the secret that had so puzzled me—he would obliterate that ugly and irregular work hole and littered dooryard, bury them beneath his mound of earth and, working from within, would make a new and neater outlet somewhere through the turf nearby."

What was its front entrance now becomes no entrance at all, and there will be a new front entrance, or several of them. These may be hidden beneath rocks, logs, or woodpiles toward which the chipmunk has dug its tunnel. No earth has been moved through them and there is scarcely any sign to attract the attention of nosy predators. If the chipmunk wants to protect itself further from snakes and weasels that might come into its tunnel, it can plug up these entrances too.

Most tunnels are home to only one adult chipmunk, although more than one may live in the same burrow during the winter.

Unlike some animals that spend their winters in hiding, the chipmunk does not build up a thick layer of fat. Neither is it likely to drift into a state of true hibernation. During the very coldest weather it may curl up deep in its burrow, its nose against its hind feet and its tail snug over its feet and head. There it sleeps so heavily that it seems to hibernate. The body temperature falls somewhat and the heart beat slows. But if the little squirrel gets hungry, it awakens.

During March we often see the chipmunks out of their burrows for a first look at spring. The breeding season comes late in March. After mating, the female will carry her young for thirty-two days before they are born. There are usually four of them in a litter.

The chipmunks are completely helpless when born, so small and thin they seem almost transparent. Their tiny bodies are naked, their eyes closed, ears sealed. Gradually they acquire a thin covering of fur. But their eyes remain closed until they are thirty-five days old and during that time they must stay in the security of the mother's burrow.

Their first look at the bright outdoor world comes when the young ones are about two months old. They will stay with their mother through the first part of summer and are believed to leave the security of their first homes when about three months old. Then the female may have a second litter, but probably most of the time she raises only one litter each year.

A chipmunk gathering acorns and stuffing them into its cheek pouches.

Autumn is the time of harvest and during the weeks when the forest leaves change from green to reds, yellows, and browns, the chipmunks are hurrying around gathering food that will help them through the rapidly approaching winter.

There are many delicacies that appeal to the chipmunk's tastes, and a list of foods eaten by these miniature squirrels would include beetles, grubs, birds' eggs, grain, wild fruits, berries, mushrooms, snails, and slugs. Blackberries and raspberries are a special treat for the chipmunk and when these berries are ripe, it may eat only dessert, one helping of fruit after the other. It cuts through the shell of snails and extracts the tender meat. It pounces on butterflies that may be hovering over mud puddles and consumes them quickly. And if the chipmunk encounters a snake that is small enough, it may attack it with the ferocity of the mongoose, kill it, and dine on snake meat. This seems fair enough in view of the fact that larger snakes often eat chipmunks.

But nuts are the choice food for the chipmunk, especially for its winter meals. Beechnuts and acorns are special favorites, and when these delicacies are ripe in fall, the long days are filled with gathering and rushing off with them to the chipmunk's burrow.

The chipmunk saves time in its harvest because it has special storage pouches in its cheeks. Although these pouches are not lined with hair, they are dry on the inside. Into them go as many seeds or nuts as the chipmunk can pack away. Instead of wasting energy by rushing off to its burrow with each new nut it discovers, it fills its pouches until its face is puffed out on both sides and it seems to suffer from the world's worst case of mumps. When there is no room for more, it scampers off along its secret trail, headed for home with its treasure.

This can go on for hours if the food supplies are good. Sometimes the chipmunk does not know when to stop and may store far more food than it needs for the winter. Naturalists have reported chipmunks carrying at one time as many as 31 big yellow kernels of corn in its pouches or 145 grains of wheat. This may equal two heaping tablespoonsful of food. The pouches will hold more than 60 sunflower seeds.

John Burroughs once offered one of his favorite chipmunks a supply of corn plus four quarts of hickory nuts. All of these went down to the bedroom below. The next day the squirrel took two more quarts of hickory nuts. By the end of the week it had carted off seven quarts of hickory nuts and chestnuts. By this time it seemed less eager to store more food; and while other chipmunks still scoured the forest for winter supplies, the lucky chipmunk

A chipmunk with its cheek pouches full.
Note the chipmunk's long, sharp incisors.

practically stopped carrying nuts. Perhaps it had run out of storage space.

Because the chipmunk may awaken from hunger during the winter months, it must have food handy down in its burrow. The chipmunk stores the food right in its bedroom, by putting nuts and acorns beneath its bed. The room is filled so high with food that the chipmunk's mattress of grass and shredded leaves and bark is up against the roof.

If it awakens hungry, the chipmunk digs down under the bed and brings up something to eat. The shells are cut off and the sweet heart of the nut satisfies its midwinter hunger. The shells are usually moved away from the bedroom and stored in another room. Gradually, as winter drags on, the chipmunk's bed drops lower and lower. But if the bedroom food supply runs low, there are more nuts stored in another chamber or two not far away.

During the warmer months some of the chipmunk's meals are consumed outdoors. Usually these outdoor meals consist of soft foods, the fruits and meat that might spoil and therefore are not suitable for underground storage. For these picnics it has a favorite perch, perhaps a stump or a rock, where it can sit and eat while keeping a sharp eye open for its enemies.

The chipmunk has good reason for staying alert. The woods and fields are the home of many creatures that would quickly eat it if they could. Long and slender weasels can chase a chipmunk right into its burrow and kill it quickly. Large snakes are also serious enemies that sometimes enter the chipmunk's underground home.

If all goes well and it meets with no serious accidents early in life, a chipmunk may live two or three years. Out in the open the chipmunk must stand constant guard against dogs, cats, and some species of hawks, as well as foxes. In the northern parts of its range it can also fall victim to the lynx and marten. All things considered, the chipmunk leads a risky life. Its world is filled with hazards, and it is perhaps good that the little squirrel has developed a nervous nature and a restless habit of casting sidelong glances at everything that moves within its field of vision. Otherwise the life of the chipmunk might be even shorter than it is.

Some people do not like chipmunks, especially when they chew on flowers or dig tunnels beneath stone steps and walks. They do not like for the lawn to get soft from a network of tunnels beneath it.

But to most people the chipmunk is a friendly creature, a sprite that adds a bright touch to the woodsy places. When treated in a friendly manner it may even come through the open door of the cabin and into the kitchen where it is offered nuts and grain. Chipmunks by nature come and go as they please, whether to gather nuts, dig tunnels, or curl up and sleep snugly through the cold winter months.

Chapter eight

~~~~~~~~~~~~~~~~~~~~~~~~~~

WOODCHUCKS

The biggest squirrels of all are the marmots. There are five species of marmots in North America. Perhaps the best known of all these is the woodchuck, known to some people as a groundhog.

Most people would recognize the woodchuck if they met it. There is no other animal except another marmot easily confused with it. It is a heavy-bodied animal that, when grown, measures from eighteen to twenty-five inches from the end of its pug nose to the tip of its short tail. It travels on short, stout legs. The ears are small and rounded. Its fur is plain gray, or brownish gray, often with white tips that make it look grizzled.

A long time ago rumors spread through the farm country that the groundhog knew a thing or two about weather forecasting. It was said the groundhog could tell when winter's cold weather would end and spring would come. All it had to do, said the legend, was waddle up out of its underground sleeping quarters and take a look around outdoors. If there was not enough sunlight for it to see its shadow, everyone could rejoice, because that meant that the back of winter had truly been broken. But if it was a bright day and there was sunlight to cast a groundhog's shadow, there was sure to be more bitter weather ahead. The groundhog,

The woodchuck is known to some people as the groundhog.

according to this story, would turn and go back to its bed, where it would stay for six more weeks of winter.

The groundhog had his own special day for making this annual weather forecast. It was February 2, a date still designated Groundhog Day on some calendars. There is only one thing wrong with the groundhog's weather forecasts, the same thing that sometimes troubles other weather forecasters—you just can't always count on their predictions coming true.

The range of the woodchuck includes much of Canada and the

eastern half of the United States, with the exception of the states of Florida and Louisiana.

In this range, the woodchuck seeking a new homesite will generally build where the soil is loose enough for easy digging but not so loose that it is likely to cave in. Besides, it wants a home in well-drained soil that will not flood easily.

The woodchuck begins a new burrow by digging a hole perpendicular to the surface. On level ground this means digging straight down. After a while the hole angles off, and it may soon turn a corner and shut the woodchuck off from the outside light. A hard-working woodchuck can dig a five-foot tunnel in a day.

This digging is done with the long claws on the woodchuck's front feet, while the teeth are used for cutting through roots. All of that loose earth has to go somewhere, so the woodchuck shoves it behind itself. It does not need to worry much about dirt getting into its ears because they have shut-off valves to close them off while it is down there digging.

This freshly excavated earth is eventually moved back to the entrance and comes flying out into the sunlight. There it falls in a heap and the woodchuck leaves it where it falls. Farmers do not approve of this, because their mowing machine cutter-bars sometimes run into the woodchuck's mounds of earth and rocks, causing the blades to break.

When the tunnel is deep enough, the woodchuck digs out a bowl-shaped bedroom at the end, usually somewhat above the level of the main tunnel. Water coming into the burrow would reach the sleeping quarters last. There the owner makes a comfortable bed of dried grass and sometimes leaves. In addition there will be other rooms, perhaps spare bedrooms and a toilet room.

Some woodchucks seem to work harder and longer on their burrows than others. They dig new tunnels and underground rooms. They create additional doorways that may be hidden in grass and brush where they are difficult to see. There may be four or five exits, giving the occupant a choice of escape routes. The completed tunnel may be forty-five feet long or more. One in Michigan was fifty-six feet long.

Living underground has several advantages for the woodchuck. Its little cellars are cool in summer, warm in winter, and pleasantly dark and quiet when the owner wants to sleep. Besides, the burrow is a safety zone into which the woodchuck can hurry at the first sign of danger.

Before coming out of its den, the woodchuck will pause and listen to hear what might be up there. Then it peers out cautiously and looks around. It comes into the open and promptly sits up to look around some more. If it sees a dog, fox, hawk, man, or other suspicious-looking creature, the woodchuck drops to all four feet and scampers back into its underground shelter.

But if all is clear, it may move off a short distance and begin eating. Woodchucks do not ordinarily go far from the safety of their burrows and live out their lives in the same den without traveling more than about a hundred yards, the length of a football field.

If an enemy surprises it and cuts off its escape route, it may climb into a tree. Woodchucks have been seen forty feet above the ground. It may even swim if forced to the water. If all else fails, it may show its long white incisors, growl, and fight its enemy. Groundhogs have sent surprised dogs home howling with badly cut ears. No one, however, should recommend to a woodchuck that it pick a fight with a dog.

Hunters sometimes shoot woodchucks with rifles and bows and arrows. But more often than not, the woodchuck spots the hunter first and disappears. One Pennsylvania hunter reported the remarkable act that saved one woodchuck from death. The animal was eating alfalfa, when it saw the hunter coming. But the wood-

Woodchucks will sometimes climb trees to escape danger.

chuck went right on eating—perhaps the food tasted so good it did not want to leave. The man walked up beside the woodchuck, expecting it to run, but it just stayed there. It looked the hunter right in the eye, and the man could not bring himself to shoot the trusting woodchuck. When he walked away, the hunter looked back several times. Each time the woodchuck was still there, and still eating.

During the summer months the woodchuck usually leads an orderly life, and like most of us, eats three meals a day, coming out to feed morning, noon, and night. Its food includes green grass and legumes and sometimes a wide variety of tender vegetables from the farmer's garden. In between meals there is not much to keep the animal busy. There is now time to take another nap, so the woodchuck goes back down to its comfortable bedroom.

Unlike many members of the squirrel family, the woodchuck does not have to store food for winter. Instead it stores fat. Toward the end of summer it grows fatter and fatter. In a single day it may eat a third of its body weight in clover and grasses. It may weigh half again as much in early fall as it did in early spring. This seems like an easy life—eat, sleep, eat, and sleep some more.

But in these last weeks of summer, the woodchuck is preparing for winter, which it passes in hibernation. As this hibernation begins, a deep sleep overcomes the woodchuck. Its life processes slow down. The hibernating animal's body is conserving energy. In summer it may have breathed 1800 times an hour, but in the dead of winter it may take only 10 or 12 breaths an hour. Meanwhile the heartbeat has slowed from 80 times a minute to perhaps 4 or 5. Even the body temperature falls lower and lower. From its usual summer level of about 100 degrees Fahrenheit, it drops to between 57 and 38 degrees, perhaps only 5 or 6 degrees above the freezing point.

This hibernation may continue for four or five months in a place the woodchuck has sealed off from the rest of the burrow. Every year the woodchuck may be only a few feet from snow but it never knows what snow looks like. All winter long the woodchuck stays curled up in bed. More than two-thirds of its life is spent either sleeping or hibernating.

What if its body temperature drops near the freezing point? The hibernating animal would die at freezing temperatures. But this has been taken care of. It is equipped with a special thermostat that warms it up to a safe level. This thermostat is a specialized tissue, known as "brown fat," that lies between the shoulder blades. This fat also increases the animal's body temperature and helps it awaken according to the schedules maintained by its biological clocks. Many mammals have a supply of this brown fat when first born. Most however, lose it. But hibernating animals keep it throughout their lives.

While the woodchuck sleeps the winter away, company may drop in for a visit. Skunks take refuge in woodchuck burrows, as do rabbits and even pheasants. Sometimes they live there all winter without the knowledge of their host.

In spring the woodchuck, considerably thinner after its winter of fasting, slowly awakens. It may need several hours to awaken fully from the long hibernation. When the male first comes from the burrow, the season of mating has arrived. During these days he makes an exception to his habit of staying close to home. He wanders about the nearby countryside visiting the females and sometimes fighting with other males encountered in the fields and along the edges of the forest.

A month after mating, in April or May in the northern states, the female gives birth to anywhere from two to nine young. The average number is four. Each of the newborn woodchucks resembles other newborn members of the squirrel family in its helplessness. It is blind and naked, pinkish in color, and about four to four-and-a-half inches long. It weighs perhaps one-and-a-half ounces, and for four weeks the mother must spend much time caring for her helpless babies.

By mid-summer, however, the young woodchucks, looking like half-size copies of their parents, come from their home burrows and waddle along with their mothers to gather some of their own food from the fields of tender green crops.

If no accident befalls the young woodchucks, if no fox, hawk, dog, or coyote catches them, and no automobile runs over them, they will leave home in mid-summer. Now they must find new territories of their own. Then they must dig a burrow and get ready for winter. The following year they will have young of their own. If all goes well for them, they may live four or five years. That does not seem long for an animal that does little but eat and sleep, and now and then add a new room to its home.

The Arctic ground squirrel is aboveground and active only during the brief summer, and the remainder of the year hibernates in its dark tunnels beneath the tundra.

Chapter nine

MORE UNDERGROUND SQUIRRELS

There are several other kinds of squirrels besides chipmunks, woodchucks, and other marmots, that live in the ground. One of these is the sik-sik, a large ground squirrel about twelve to eighteen inches long and weighing one to one-and-a-half pounds. Most of us would have to go a long way to see a sik-sik, for they live in the Arctic. Eskimos see them often. Eskimos eat these Arctic ground squirrels and use the plain reddish-brown furs to make clothing.

Sometimes in the Arctic, when traveling along a river with high banks, I have looked up and seen a sik-sik. The little squirrel sits there in the short grass, as motionless as a stake driven into the ground. It sits up straight and still against the sky, watching the boat go down the river.

Where would an animal get such a name? This squirrel names itself—"sik-sik" is what it says. Spotting a stranger in its territory, the squirrel sits up to see if the situation looks dangerous, decides yes, it does look dangerous, says "sik-sik," then gets down, and runs for its burrow.

In Mt. McKinley National Park in Alaska, some Arctic ground squirrels are very tame. I remember one that lived outside our tent in the campground above Wonder Lake. The little squirrel had learned that campers like ground squirrels. It had also learned that campers carry many good things to eat. I took its photograph while a friend of mine fed it a slice of bread from his hand. The squirrel sat up and ate as though it had forgotten that it was a wild animal, or didn't care. In Alaska this ground squirrel also says "sik-sik," but Alaskan people do not call it "sik-sik." They call it "parky" instead, because they use its fur to trim warm parkas.

People are only one of many enemies of the Arctic ground squirrel. Eagles eat them; so do hawks, foxes, wolves, wolverines, and even grizzly bears if they catch them. Grizzly bears sometimes try to dig the Arctic ground squirrel out of the ground; but this means a lot of digging for a small meal, and often the nervous ground squirrel escapes.

Because so many animals eat the Arctic ground squirrel, it is probably a good thing for the predators that these squirrels have large families. The average litter will include eight to ten young ones. They are born in early summer and four months later are full-sized. Their food is mostly grass and other vegetation, but they also eat animal matter, including insects.

These youngsters live underground for the first weeks of their lives. Their burrows help keep the Arctic ground squirrels safe. The burrow starts straight down into the ground. Then when it is three or four feet deep, or when it reaches the permafrost (the permanently frozen layer of the earth's surface), it turns off at an angle. After that it may turn again. There will be several entrances before the burrow is finished, giving the ground squirrel a choice of escapes from its enemies.

Down there in the darkness there are probably several little rooms it has dug out to make its place homelike. One is for sleeping, and it is lined with soft grass and maybe even some caribou fur that has dropped off the big Arctic deer as they passed through the squirrel's front yard.

SQUIRRELS

In this bed the ground squirrel spends its nights. It comes out to feed only during the day, and seems to like bright days better than the dark, stormy ones. It may get ready for the night by first plugging up the entrance of its burrow with earth. It also seals itself off this way when hibernating.

In the Arctic, where winters are long and bitterly cold, hibernation lasts about seven months for the ground squirrel. This is often a difficult time for the predators that eat squirrels. By late summer the squirrel has become very fat. This fat must keep its body supplied during the entire winter. By the time hibernation ends in spring it will lose almost half of this weight.

Down there, sealed off from the rest of the world, the ground squirrel goes into a very deep hibernation. Its heart, which during the summer would beat from 200 to 350 times a minute, slows down to 5 to 10 beats a minute. Breathing becomes so slow it seems the squirrel is not breathing at all. Its body temperature falls to almost freezing. If it falls below freezing the animal dies.

Outside the burrow the temperature may drop to fifty degrees below zero. But when spring comes again, the Eskimo children see the squirrels sticking their heads up out of the burrows and they hear them welcome the new season with cries of "sik-sik."

Another ground squirrel with a call that sounds almost the same lives in the central part of the United States. This squirrel can be seen in the grasslands all the way from Utah to Ohio and from southern Canada southward into Texas. It has several names. Some people call it a gopher. Others have named it the federation squirrel because it has thirteen stripes, like the first flag of the American federation of states. These stripes run up and down its back, where there are also a lot of spots. Some people, looking at the stripes, call the animal the thirteen-striped ground squirrel.

Whatever you call it, the striped ground squirrel is a most un-

A thirteen-lined ground squirrel, also known
as a federation squirrel and a gopher.

usual animal. In some ways it is like its cousin up in the land of
the Eskimos—it digs elaborate burrows, it hibernates, and it has
big families.

This squirrel reaches a size of ten to twelve inches, with the tail
accounting for about a third of its length. It has short legs and is a
rather slender creature. The males and females are marked alike
with their brownish fur and yellowish brown stripes and spots. The
male, however, is slightly bigger than the female.

Its burrows are often difficult for people to find. One reason is
that the entrances may be hidden in clumps of grass. Another is
that the soil the squirrel digs to make its burrow is not dumped
carelessly outside the entrance where it will be a tip-off to hungry
foxes, badgers, and snakes. Instead the striped ground squirrel

The Mexican ground squirrel, closely related to the thirteen-lined ground squirrel, may be seen in the United States in southern Texas.

packs the soil into its cheek pouches and carries it away. It spreads this soil on nearby grassy places, scattering the evidence around where it will not be seen. And, like the Artic ground squirrel, it often plugs up the entrances to its burrow from the inside.

The striped ground squirrel has many enemies besides people. The hawks that prey on them include the marsh hawk, red-tailed hawk, Cooper's hawk, and sparrow hawk. Foxes, bobcats, and coyotes all try to catch them. The badger is a special enemy because it can dig the striped ground squirrel right out of its burrow.

People sometimes have trouble making up their minds whether they like this squirrel or not. They like it when it eats insects, and they like it a lot when it eats mice; but when it includes wheat and oats in its diet, people like the striped squirrel less. Before they drove modern machinery, farmers left their wheat standing in shocks in the field. Then the striped ground squirrel often ended its burrow right under a shock of wheat. This not only made a good hiding place, but it also brought the squirrel right up where it could harvest the golden grains of wheat and hardly leave home. Sometimes it carries grain, as well as other seeds, down into its burrow and stores the food there for later use. In this way it may store thousands of grains of wheat or oats.

More Underground Squirrels

Chapter ten

PRAIRIE DOGS

On a sunny afternoon we drove into the hills of Wind Cave National Park in South Dakota, searching for wild animals to photograph. The rolling, open countryside was carpeted with short prairie grasses, and prairie flowers were blooming.

Across the ridge a giant black buffalo bull wandered peacefully along, stopping now and then to cut himself another mouthful of grass. Nearby, a curious pronghorn antelope and her two fawns stood in the grass, staring up the hill at us. But most of the visitors hardly noticed the splendid bison or the fleet-footed antelope. They were watching instead a community of fat, little brown animals that ran about on short legs. The animals sat up frequently, looked at the world around them, and barked at intruders. I soon began stalking these little prairie dogs with my camera.

By moving slowly and cautiously, I managed to photograph these remarkable little creatures. A mother and her three fat youngsters nosed about the prairie, having their breakfast of grass. Another prairie dog looked at me, then stood on the mound at the entrance of its burrow, lifted its face up, and barked. Others stopped and looked around, but went back to what they were doing. Nearby, an old, fat prairie dog sat half-asleep in the warm

A black-tailed prairie dog in Wind Cave National Park.

sunlight at the entrance to its burrow. This was the usual neighborhood activity on a nice day.

Prairie dogs are not dogs at all, but squirrels instead. Early explorers called them dogs because they barked so much. Frenchmen who came to North America called this animal *petite chien*, which means "little dog."

There are two species of prairie dogs. One has a black tip on its tail and consequently is known as the "black-tailed prairie dog." This is the one we met in Wind Cave National Park. It once lived on the broad grasslands from North Dakota southward to Texas, then west to Arizona and Montana. Today it survives in only small parts of this range.

Its cousin, the white-tailed prairie dog, is not so famous. This prairie dog, less numerous than the black-tailed species, lives in the mountains, in the grassy meadows above 6,000 feet elevation. Its tail has a white tip.

Black-tailed prairie dogs are easy to recognize. You will know them because they live close together. Besides, they have circular mounds around the entrances to their burrows. They are about the size of a small housecat, about one foot long, and weigh from two to three pounds. They have a tail that is three or four inches long. Their fur is reddish-brown or gray colored.

Once, a hundred years ago, travelers through the western plains would have had no trouble finding prairie dogs. They might even have seen a million of them. In 1853, John R. Bartlett traveled across Texas for three days, covering about twenty miles each day. He was in the same prairie dog town every hour of that trip. Their burrows, he said, were only about thirty feet apart. He figured that more than 50 million prairie dogs lived in this one town.

Dr. C. Hart Merriam, once director of the United States Biological Survey, was amazed at the numbers of prairie dogs he found in Texas in 1900. One prairie dog town stretched on and on until Dr. Merriam thought it might be 100 miles wide and 250 miles long. How many of the little grass eaters would be crowded into this megalopolis? Dr. Merriam thought there might be 400 million. No one will ever know how many prairie dogs there were in all of North America in those times.

Before men brought large herds of cattle to the grasslands, the black-tailed prairie dogs had wild neighbors that were important to them, especially the buffalo. These huge, lumbering creatures kept the grass eaten off short and the earth packed solid, which made good living conditions for prairie dogs. Where the grass was short, they could see their enemies.

Then man came with their herds of cattle. This was bad for the prairie dogs because, except for occasional insects, they ate ex-

This prairie dog family has come out of their burrow to eat grass.

actly the same thing that the cows needed—grass. For the cattle-men the choice was an easy one—get rid of the prairie dogs.

How do you remove millions of prairie dogs from the open range? You feed them a food they cannot resist. You scatter grain through their towns, after first covering the grain with poison. The prairie dogs die. Their towns grow quiet. The grass grows and the cattle eat. In a few years the old burrows fill up and are gone and nobody can tell where the prairie dogs once stuck their heads out to see if all was safe.

Some years ago businessmen in Greeley, Colorado, decided they wanted more prairie dogs. There was a little colony of the animals nearby, but most of them had been killed with guns and poisons. Tourists and local people, too, liked to watch them, however. The businessmen decided that maybe they could find some wild prairie dogs and bring them to Greeley.

About ten miles away, along the Thompson River, lived some prairie dogs. The question was how to get them to move closer to Greeley. As soon as you try to catch a prairie dog, it dashes off to its burrow and hides down there, deep in the earth. Besides, it barks a sharp warning to all its neighbors first, sending them hurrying home, and there is not a prairie dog in sight. Their burrows are too deep and complicated to dig the animals out.

First the Colorado prairie dog catchers thought they could flood the burrows and grab the squirrels when they came up for air. But the idea did not work out very well. Barrels of water were poured down one prairie dog hole and it still did not fill up. Then the men took out a tank truck that carried 2,400 gallons and began running this water down into the prairie dog hole. That should bring him up!

But it didn't. Instead all the water went into the earth and some of it began spouting up from another hole thirty feet away. The prairie dog chasers decided the little animals had so many places to hide down there in their caverns that flooding would never get them out.

They also tried box traps. These failed too. They were about to give up the whole project and do without any new prairie dogs when one man, a fisherman in his spare time, had a brilliant idea. Why not go fishing for prairie dogs?

They took their spinning rods and reels and headed for the dog town. There they arranged the ends of their lines in loops with slip knots. Each loop was placed carefully around an entrance into which a prairie dog had vanished. Prairie dogs are curious animals. Before long they were poking their heads out to see if the strangers were still around and what they were doing if they were. As the prairie dogs came out, fishing lines tightened around them.

After much scuffling, the captured prairie dogs were safely transferred to boxes for the ride to their new home.

The businessmen felt that they had performed a good deed. Perhaps they had. But the story had a sad ending. The ranch where the prairie dogs were released was sold, and the new owner wanted no prairie dogs. So the prairie dog town was poisoned.

Prairie dogs dig remarkable tunnels in which to live. The burrow opens into a hallway that goes straight down for several feet. The tunneling rodent, standing on its head, loosens the earth with its front feet and teeth, then kicks the soil up behind it. Then the plan calls for the tunnel to make a right angle turn. But each prairie dog may have its own design and each burrow may be different from all the others. There are usually short tunnels off the main stem and these often end in special rooms.

The prairie dog nearly always includes in its house plan a small side room a few feet below the surface. This is its guard room. Whenever a predator chases the prairie dog, the escaping animal scurries down into its burrow, then stops at its guard room. There it sits and listens. Also, when it heads outside from its cool, dark bedroom, it pauses in the guard room, where it listens some more. In addition, this guard room gives the prairie dog a good place to escape high water.

Other rooms have various purposes. The bedroom will be outfitted with a mattress of soft fine grass. And there is a special room for a toilet.

One feature the black-tailed prairie dog's home will have is a ring of earth mounded around the entrance.

After the prairie dog has scattered the freshly dug earth on the mound, it must tamp it down tightly. For this the animal uses both its feet and its nose, tamping and pounding until the earth is firm.

This doughnut-shaped mound serves as protection against high water. Out on the level land where many prairie dogs live, the

A fat black-tailed prairie dog sits on the mound outside its burrow.

rains may not come often, but when they do they may be heavy. A genuine gully washer may send sheets of water washing across the plains. When this water flows through a dog town, the dikes around the entrances keep it out of the burrows. Evolution favors the prairie dogs that are good engineers. Lazy animals that neglect building good mounds may have fewer young surviving the rainstorms.

In addition, the mounds are prairie dog "patios." Sitting up on its mound the barking squirrel can study its world; and if an enemy comes it is only a couple of steps to safety.

These plains dwellers have many enemies. Rattlesnakes seeking a snug place to hibernate may move into prairie dog burrows and may still be around in early summer to eat young prairie dogs. Little, round-faced burrowing owls find the diggings of the prairie dog ideal for their own use. These are the only plains birds that nest underground. And not only do they invade the prairie dog's burrow, but they also feast occasionally on its young.

Another creature that runs freely through the underground home of the prairie dog is the black-footed ferret. But these long, slender animals with their short legs and black masks are now so rare that most prairie dogs have never seen one. The ferret is endangered because poisoning has killed off its prey, the prairie dog.

The prairie dog has always had to watch closely for the coyote and the badger. The badger is a champion digger and in a matter of minutes it can dig a hidden prairie dog out of its burrow. As if this is not enough, the coyote sometimes tags along with the badger. While the badger is down there digging, brother coyote waits patiently up at the entrance. Once in a while a frantic prairie dog will be fortunate enough to get past the burrowing badger and scamper up into the sunshine. But there he finds the quick-moving coyote waiting.

Even when the badger is not around, the coyote is eager to feast on a fat prairie dog. Catching a prairie dog away from its burrow, however, is not easy for the coyote. There are many stories about how the coyote outwits the prairie dog. One that seems logical tells of the method two coyotes can use by working together. They approach the prairie dog town with one coyote trotting along close behind the other, trying to stay hidden behind its mate. The prairie dogs stand up on their hind legs and bark and scold loudly. Word flashes through the whole community. Coyote in town! Prairie dogs everywhere dash for their burrows. The coyotes trot right on into town. The lead coyote leaps lightly over the top of the first prairie dog burrow and trots on slowly. But its mate has stopped on the edge of the mound and lies there crouched low against the ground to wait. Curious, the prairie dog comes up on the mound to watch the coyote pass on to a safe distance. It never thinks to look behind itself, however, and in that instant the second coyote grabs it.

Red-tailed hawks, rough-legged hawks, and golden eagles also patrol the prairie dog towns, alert for the careless one caught too far from home.

Prairie dogs subdivide their towns so that each animal has its own community. It knows the borders of its neighborhood and within these boundaries is welcome. But it is not free to roam around town and go into strange neighborhoods. If it does, fights break out. The wandering prairie dog rushes back home to familiar territory.

About the last of March the tempo of living picks up throughout the dog town. This is the mating season. Males travel more and seek out the females. Some of the females mate during their first year, the others when two years old. They average four to six young in each litter, with young mothers usually having fewer young. Their young are born about a month after mating.

By the time they are seven or eight weeks old, and the summer days have turned warm and pleasant, the little prairie dogs are seen up in the grasslands with their parents. The growing grass nourishes them well, and they are ready for weaning in September. This is the time when the mothers of many wild animals send their young out into the world on their own for the first time.

But the female prairie dog has a different plan. Instead, *she* leaves home. She either finds an old burrow to occupy or begins digging a new one. Her young ones stay on in the home burrow. Then, by autumn, they also disperse, each one seeking a burrow of its own.

These creatures of the western grasslands, once sitting outside their burrows by the millions, are diminishing in number. Ranchers still call in government technicians to help them rid their pastures of the last little communities of prairie dogs. Prairie dog towns vanish one by one. The black-tailed prairie dog is one member of the squirrel family that does not have a promising future.

INDEX